MILLWALL
50
GREATEST
MATCHES

First published in Great Britain in 2011 by The Derby Books Publishing Company Limited, Derby, DE21 4SZ.

This edition published in Great Britain in 2013 by DB Publishing, an imprint of JMD Media Ltd

ISBN 978-1-78091-297-4

Printed and bound in the UK by Copytech (UK) Ltd Peterborough

DAVID SULLIVAN

MILLWALL

50

GREATEST MATCHES

Contents

INTRODUCTION

Choosing these 50 matches has been enjoyable and though some readers might not agree with this selection I have tried to be as discerning as possible and have attempted to maintain a situation where a majority of older Millwall supporters, and those a bit younger will have cause to remember most of these matches.

Within, it records one of Millwall's best away victories over Tottenham in 1900 and the equally outstanding result in 1929 against the same opposition. The same decade saw the superb performances at Bradford City, a game that was threatened by a snow storm and the Lions' only victory so far over Manchester United.

The thrilling FA Cup tie at The Den with Leicester City in 1934, a display that should have given Millwall the impetus to avoid relegation, in which they subsequently failed. However, the thumping of Manchester City at Maine Road in 1938 was one of the stand-out pre-war results.

Following hostilities the game many old-timers like to recall is the defeat of mighty Newcastle United in 1957 in which Millwall, against all odds won through. There are two classic encounters with Port Vale at The Den in 1958 and 1962, but the 1960 clash with Chester was drifting aimlessly along until a six-goal burst in the last 20 minutes or so, gave the game a totally false impression.

Concluding the 'Swinging Sixties' three matches against Middlesbrough, Carlisle United and Sheffield United went to show how much Millwall's vociferous crowd could influence the outcome of game by their unremitting backing. Drubbing is word that comes to mind, when Birmingham in 1970 and Swindon Town a decade later were both beaten 6–2, to top and tail some excellent games like the splendid draw with Wolves on a wet New Year's Day 1977.

The high-scoring 5–4 defeat at Exeter in 1981 came in a period of flux for the Lions as they struggled to find consistency. But by 1988 they had arrived at the top table, and duly won their initial First Division home game against Derby County. Later that season came the memorable and unforgettable televised classic against Norwich City. When the move to new ground occurred in 1993 Millwall reached a level that even their most optimistic fan never thought the Lions would aspire to.

The New Den would witness five Divisional Play-offs, a fine run that would eventually see Millwall reach their first FA Cup Final in 2004 and their first ever foray into European football against Ferencvaros. The Mother's Day massacre of West Ham United and latterly the Titanic struggles with Leeds United. An added bonus was the two Wembley appearances in 2009 and 2010.

All in all following the Lions over three decades has been a roller coaster ride that has not only excited but also brought despair. Nonetheless, it illustrates what a great and unique football club Millwall are.

David Sullivan
June 2011

Acknowledgements

In compiling this latest volume on the Lions I have again utilised the services of Brian Tonks the official Millwall photographer and my fellow historian Chris Bethell whose own archive of pictures once again came to my rescue, and in rapid time I might add. To them both I will be eternally grateful.

Another trusted and reliable friend I must mention is Mike Bondy who expertise in obtaining the odd match report made my task a lot easier. Thanks must also go to Alex Morton and Jo Rush at DB Publishing for their assistance throughout and for bringing my labours to a conclusion.

Lastly, the biggest thank you goes to all the Millwall players down the years who have made it possible for me to put their deeds into words.

1

TOTTENHAM HOTSPUR V MILLWALL ATHLETIC

1 September 1900   **Southern League**
White Hart Lane, London   **Attendance: 13,400**

Following the exploits in the FA Cup when they reached their first semi-final the previous season, Millwall Athletic now looked ahead to a campaign in which they would not only attempt to build upon their newly acquired fame, but also to secure their position as one of the leading clubs in the south of England. But there was a fly in the ointment: the lease on the ground was due to expire and, with the expected expansion of the Millwall Docks, there was no likelihood of it being renewed. The sword of Damocles was hovering menacingly over the very existence of the club. With all the surrounding uncertainty, the team embarked upon what could be Millwall Athletic's final season.

The gloomy forecast was made worse for the supporters when the likes of John Brearley left with Charlie Burgess and Edward Allen, known as Ned.

A new team group for season 1900/01 which contains the 11 who beat Tottenham on the opening day. Back row (left to right): F. Griffiths, H. Shutt, W. Millar, T. Joyce, T. Davidson, E. Moor (groundsman). Middle row: A. Hunter (trainer), E.R. Stopher (team manager), G. Henderson, A.T. Millar, H. Banks, W. Davis, G.A. Saunders (director). Front row: W. Dryburgh, J. Sharples, S. Caie, A. Carnelly, T. Wilson.

Also departing the scene was the excellent goalkeeper Walter Cox and the equally talented Hugh Goldie. Coming into the mix was a trio of recruits from Swindon Town in right-back Hartley Shutt, the half-back George Henderson and winger Tommy Wilson.

But whatever lay around the corner, the club's problems were forgotten for 90 minutes when the side responded in an excellent manner for the visit to North London. Sweet revenge indeed, as Millwall went one better by cancelling out Tottenham's victory on the opening day at the East Ferry Road the previous season. But this success was fully deserved as Millwall sparkled in attack and were quicker to the ball, and had it not been for George Clawley in the Tottenham goal, the outcome would have been more of an embarrassment for the home team.

The Tottenham forwards were pretty ineffective for the majority of the match, and as such never created any clear-cut chances to threaten the Millwall goal. Tottenham's demise was down to the tone set by the visitors early on, a tone that saw them take the lead soon after kick-off. It was Scot, Sandy Caie, who set outside-left Tom Wilson on his way down the flank, before a tackle from Tottenham's Tom Morris momentarily held Millwall at bay, but John Cameron's failure to control the ball from a throw-on saw Millwall regain possession through skipper Arthur Millar. Quickly switching play to Willy Dryburgh out on the right flank, the little winger took Millar's pass and gave Joe Sharples, the fourth summer capture from Swindon Town, the easy task of shooting past Clawley for Sharples's first goal in a Millwall shirt. The endeavours of Tottenham's Sandy Brown to bring his team back into contention found the Millwall defence in an uncompromising mood, as Spurs struggled to build any sort of momentum. Therefore it came as no surprise when Millwall scored again. The ever-increasing influence of Millar and his fellow Scot George Henderson was to become a constant threat to the Tottenham defence, where Melia was suffering a torrid afternoon. Millar and Henderson created an ingenious move for Caie to outfox the wretched Melia and Clawley to snap up Millwall's second goal.

Despite the setbacks, Tottenham's enthusiasm never waned, and for what was left of the first half they produced some of their best football. But when a hint of promise arose, their hopes were immediately crushed, for they were continuously led up blind alleys. In the rare event of Tottenham getting a sight of the Millwall goal, they found goalkeeper John 'Tiny' Joyce to be an insurmountable obstacle. Tiny's presence and Millwall's defensive qualities were two of the main reasons why Spurs left the field at the interval two goals in arrears.

Tottenham's spirited and aggressive start saw them dominate in the early stages of the second 45 minutes, during which time both Brown and Cameron came close to reducing the lead, but their inability to loosen Millwall's vice-like grip, even during such a spurt of dynamism, made them vulnerable to the counter-attack.

Goalkeeper John 'Tiny' Joyce who kept a clean record against Spurs but lost his place to Fred Griffiths for the rest of the campaign when he let in seven goals at Bristol City two months later.

It was one such attack in the 70th minute that caused Spurs's resistance to break and allowed Millwall to claim a third goal. The build-up was entirely of Caledonian manufacture and was initiated by another new addition to the team, the former Bury full-back Tom Davidson. The gangly Scot, who had collected an FA Cup winner's medal with Bury the previous season, was carrying a slight injury, but it did not impair his ability to send a peach of a pass up to Caie. With one graceful touch and a canny dribble, the centre-forward paved the way for his compatriot, Dryburgh, to beat Clawley with a rasping drive from a fair way out.

The Dockers finished the Southern League in fourth position and were the only team to win at Tottenham that season. Spurs would follow Millwall into fifth place, although Millwall's victory over the Lilywhites would be brief; Spurs would have something to smile about the following April when they became the first professional club outside the Football League to lift the FA Cup.

For Millwall though, the future looked bright after the directors concluded an agreement to lease a new ground for the start of 1901–2 season. The ground would be simply known as North Greenwich.

What do you think of the Dark Blues now?
What do you think of the boys?
The Spurs they thought them duffers,
But now it's them that suffers,
And they don't think them duffers now.

Anon-*East End News*

Tottenham Hotspur 0   Millwall Athletic 3
                             Sharples, Caie, Dryburgh.

Tottenham Hotspur: Clawley, Melia, Tait, Morris, McNaught, Stormont, Smith, Cameron, Brown, Pangbourne, Kirwan.
Millwall Athletic: Joyce, Shutt, Davidson, Henderson, Millar, Banks, Dryburgh, Sharples, Caie, Carnelly, Wilson.

MILLWALL V

FULHAM

15 February 1904   **London League**
North Greenwich, London   **Attendance: 1,200**

In the early days of their history, Millwall set a precedent of winning many of the competitions they entered at the first attempt, but one competition to elude them was the London League, which came into existence for the 1901–2 season and then comprised of just eight matches. By the time Millwall succeeded in winning the title in 1904, the League had been extended to 12 fixtures, in which Millwall would win 11 and draw the other, leaving them unbeaten in what was the third and final campaign of the competition.

Having beaten Fulham in the Southern League on the previous Saturday at Craven Cottage, Millwall would now entertain the West Londoners in the London League. Victorious in five out of five of the matches in this particular tournament, the Lions realised that if they could maintain their winning run they would have a splendid opportunity to lift the title. With this in mind, Millwall fielded an unchanged team from that which had secured a 2–1 success 48 hours earlier. Fulham, however, played a weak

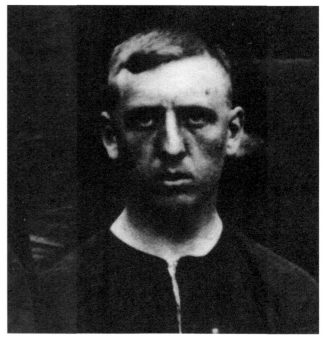

team, and as a consequence suffered a crushing defeat.

The points were virtually guaranteed after Millwall raced into a quick-fire three-goal lead. The first goal was set up by a Willie Maxwell pass, which found the exuberant Harry Astley. After drawing both Fulham full-backs out of position, Astley found the room to rocket his shot past Billy Biggar in the Fulham goal after three minutes.

The second goal arrived when the former Scottish cap, Maxwell, finished off a fine Astley and Dick Jones move. Moments later it was 3–0 when Astley terminated his marvellous solo run with an equally devastating finish for his second goal and Millwall's third. Fulham's Jack Hamilton kept the action going with another fine goal to reduce the deficit after 35 minutes, when he skilfully lifted the ball over a posse of players following a corner for a consolation goal.

As he had on the Saturday, Willie Maxwell hit another brace against the Cottagers when he converted a cross from Welsh international Ernie Watkins on the stroke of half-time. Within two minutes of the restart, Astley completed his hat-trick following another superb solo effort. The ex-Bolton Wanderer then took his tally to four in a similar style, as a ragged Fulham side began to sink without trace. By the time Millwall's Welsh duo of Dick Jones and Ernie Watkins completed the rout, the visitors were well and truly thrashed. The crowd had been treated to an extravaganza of excellent attacking football on a day when the unusually fine weather mirrored an equally spectacular display. The victory drew Millwall level at the top of the table with Woolwich Arsenal, who had played two games more than Millwall.

Millwall 8   Fulham 1
Astley (4),   Hamilton
Maxwell (2),
Watkins, Jones R.

Millwall: Joyce, Easton, Stevenson, Riley, McLean J., Millar, Moran, Maxwell, Astley, Jones R., Watkins.
Fulham: Biggar, Harwood, Nidd, Green, Hamilton, Colville, Sear, Connor, Robotham, Axcell, Anderson.

London League	P	W	D	L	F	A	PTS	POS
	12	11	1	0	37	8	23	1

3

MILLWALL V NORTHAMPTON TOWN

15 September 1919
The Den, London

Southern League
Attendance: 6,000

They say that all good things come to an end, and after 22 seasons and as one of the founding members of the Southern League, the Lions would bid farewell to a well-established institution. They and their opponents, Northampton Town, along with the rest of the senior Southern League clubs, would a year hence be opposing one another as members of the Football League's new Third Division.

This encounter would turn out to be a personal triumph for Millwall's centre-forward, the much-travelled Jimmy Broad, with the supreme opportunist claiming all four goals in the Lions' victory. The game kicked off on a dull and overcast evening, which was immediately brightened up when Millwall scored in the first minute. A burst from Boyd Mayson, one of three Millwall players to have served with the Canadian army during

Centre Forward Jimmy Broad amassed an excellent 32 goals in Millwall's last season in the Southern League, but his only hat-trick for the Lions came when he scored all four against the Cobblers.

World War One, got away down the left to put over a tantalising cross, to find Broad steaming in to place a fine header past Smith for the opener. From the restart, Town's Bellamy forced his way through, only to shoot straight at Lions 'keeper Harry Bailey. Not one to be overshadowed, Jim showed his opponent how to do it in the 20th minute by placing his low drive firmly into Smith's net to make it 2–0. Shortly afterwards, Jim thumped another chance against the crossbar, before a sprightly Northampton rallied to reduce the lead. Their chance came after a bout of pressure on the Lions, during which Bailey denied them on two other occasions before Manning beat him in the 35th minute. Unfortunately, Northampton's spurt of energy came at a time when the Lions were without skipper Joe Wilson, who was receiving some touch-line treatment.

It was a bright start to the second half for both teams, but one cohesive move saw the Cobblers draw level in the 49th minute. The build-up forced an error in the Lions rearguard and Whitworth scored from what seemed an impossible angle. The goal brought a simmering game nicely to the boil.

Millwall intensified their assaults on the Northampton goal and their efforts were to pay rich dividends, with Broad claiming a hat-trick on 60 minutes. Millwall forged further ahead two minutes later when the all-action Broad put the icing on the cake with his fourth goal of the game. His shot followed an excellent pinpoint cross from outside-right Dave Adams, which allowed Jim to head home an exquisite goal.

Jimmy Broad went on to score an amazing 32 goals from 39 games in that final Southern League season, but it was surprising that he never scored another hat-trick in this particular competition.

Millwall 4   Northampton Town 2
Broad (4)   Manning, Whitworth

Millwall: Bailey, Fort, Hill, Voisey, Wilson, McAlpine, Adams, Noble, Broad, Thomson, Mayson.
Northampton Town: Smith, Sproston, Davies, Grendon, Manning, Tomkins, Goldie, Bellamy, Whitworth, Lockett, Freeman.

4

MILLWALL V

LUTON TOWN

27 December 1926   **Third Division South**
The Den, London   **Attendance: 25,000**

Revenge was definitely in the air at the Den for the return encounter with Luton Town. The end result was a remarkable transformation from the 6–0 thrashing at Luton two days earlier, where a number of the Millwall team had completely lost the plot and, ultimately, the match. Millwall now had an opportunity to make up for the Christmas Day debacle, and to help do so they introduced Archie Gomm and Alf Black for the indisposed Alf Moule and Sid Gore, who both sustained injuries at Luton.

The strong-arm tactics supposedly used in an unsporting manner by Millwall at Luton may have been borne out, as Black, Phillips and Bryant went about their business of softening up the visitors in the early stages. But, in truth, Luton were completely outplayed; the loss of centre-forward Reid after just 20 minutes hardly helped their cause, but it could not explain a desperately poor showing.

Apart from Harper in the Hatters goal, Luton did not stand a chance. Millwall went for the jugular from the start, with the opening goal arriving

Alf Amos put Millwall on their way to avenge the Christmas Day thrashing at Luton when he opened the scoring in the 16th minute.

in the 16th minute. It was Alf Amos, who had an unhappy time at Luton, set himself up to fire in a long-range effort that went through a ruck of players and into the net. Within two minutes, following a melee, Wilf Phillips scored, before Gomm added a third shortly afterwards, virtually making Millwall's victory certain.

The form of Millwall's leader, Dick Parker, throughout was that of a man at the top of his game, and it was he who scored the fourth goal. He doubled his tally in the 50th minute when he converted Gomm's pass. Gomm then scored the sixth from close quarters, before livewire Phillips delivered the knockout blow when racing through and planting the ball past Harper for goal number seven.

Millwall's five-star performance was no way exaggerated by the result at Cold Blow Lane. In the space of 48 hours Millwall had suffered their heaviest defeat and then claimed their biggest win of the season.

Millwall 7   Luton Town 0
Amos, Phillips (2),
Gomm (2), Parker (2)

Millwall: Lansdale, Fort, Hill, Amos, Bryant, Graham, Chance, Gomm, Parker, Phillips, Black.
Luton Town: Harper, Graham, Till, Black, Rennie, Millar, Pointon, Thomson N., Reid, Woods, Thompson J.

5

MILLWALL V
COVENTRY CITY

19 November 1927
The Den, London

Third Division South
Attendance: 10,000

For the second time in what became a triumphant 1927–28 campaign, Millwall recorded a 9–1 victory when defeating Coventry City. In the days leading up to the match, Millwall added to what was an already potent squad with the capture of former England international Jack Cock from Plymouth Argyle. Jack was to make a stunning debut against City and his contribution went a long way towards the Lions obtaining an avalanche of goals. Incredible as it may seem, the score stood at 1–1 at the break, and it was Coventry who had the temerity to open the scoring in the 22nd minute; City was awarded a free-kick, and their Scottish forward, Peter Ramage, thumped home a piledriver from 30 yards to stun the home crowd into silence. But the groans of the home spectators were all forgotten by the end of the 90 minutes, as Millwall would go on to steamroller their opponents into submission. Just two minutes before half-time, Alf Black's cross was met by John Landells's head to restore parity.

John Landells brought his seasons total to 14 goals with four goals in the Coventry game, and in a record breaking season the Lions scored an amazing 87 goals at The Den.

The second half would not only see Cock's sublime influence on the game, but also an unprecedented spree of five goals in 11 minutes. Most of the visitors' good work of the first half was jettisoned in a period of mayhem that began when Landells outpaced Alex Fergus to Cock's splendid through ball and forced it past Harry Stanford to give the Lions the lead in the 47th minute.

The score became 3–1 when Jack Cock crowned a cracking first game by cashing in on a misunderstanding between Stanford and Jock Ramage. Before everyone had got their breath back, Landells claimed another two goals in a minute to register his second hat-trick of the season. The Lions were now running amok, and when Fergus's feeble attempt to tackle Black failed, Wilf 'Peanut' Phillips was there to register the sixth goal after 56 minutes.

The lull, if you can call it one, for a thoroughly devastated Coventry team barely lasted 10 minutes. Wilf Phillips began the second phase of attack to acquire Millwall's seventh goal following a fine solo run through a fast-evaporating City defence. The Den's new hero, the classy Jack Cock, whose all-round quality in leading the attack added goal number eight 15 minutes from time, before the giant Albert 'Mick' Collins completed the deluge with a header.

Despite seeing a game of wonderful football in which every Millwall player was at the top of his game, there was significant displeasure in the stands when Phillips had what would have been a 10th goal disallowed for offside, which really irked sections of the crowd. There is just no satisfying some people.

Millwall 9   Coventry City 1
Landells (4), Cock (2),   Ramage P.
Phillips (2), Collins

Millwall: Lansdale, Fort, Hill, Amos, Collins, Graham, Chance, Landells, Cock, Phillips, Black.
Coventry City: Stanford, Fergus, Ramage J., Brown, Hickman, Bird, Johnson, Heathcote, Johnstone, Ramage P., Herbert.

6

MILLWALL V TOTTENHAM HOTSPUR

2 February 1929   **Second Division**
The Den, London   **Attendance: 25,000**

In what was a stop-start initial campaign in the Second Division, Millwall finally found their feet at the end of January with a win in a nine-goal thriller at Notts County, which was a prelude to six consecutive League victories, including this dismantling of Tottenham Hotspur.

It was following their departure in controversial circumstances from the midweek FA Cup replay at Crystal Palace (where eight goals were scored) that Millwall pitched up for another London derby, this time against Spurs in their first ever visit to Cold Blow Lane, and one that they would never forget. The match saw Millwall wreak their Selhurst Park injustices on the North Londoners; the Lions were to show their celebrated guests that the winning of the Third Division South title the previous term was no flash in the pan.

Gallaher's Cigarettes.

WM. I. BRYANT
MILLWALL

Millwall's England amateur centre-half W.I. [Billy] Bryant helped himself to eight goals during the season, including a brace against Tottenham.

The comfort of an early goal certainly helped the Lions to gain confidence, but the inspirational performance of amateur Billy Bryant was also a contributing factor in an exceptional Millwall display. It was this goliath who opened the scoring after four minutes when he confidently abandoned his defensive duties and raced into the Spurs area to smash a loose ball home.

Tottenham's inevitable response saw Frank Osborne force the first of three successive corners, which were all cleared, before Arthur 'Darkie' Lowdell's stunning effort was tipped over by Lions 'keeper Joe Lansdale. Millwall retaliated with an excellent move that resulted in a penalty when George Chance's cross was needlessly handled by Matt Forster; it was left to Johnny Readman to convert the spot-kick.

Millwall's second goal was the straw that broke the camel's back, and it surprised no one when they added a third after a centre from Alf Black found the prolific John Landells to head home. Totally bemused and crestfallen, Tottenham then leaked a fourth after a quartet of point-blank efforts were miraculously blocked by a creaking Tottenham defence, until Belgium-born Bryant registered with another finely placed drive.

Reeling from a first half onslaught, Spurs nearly conceded a fifth goal at the start of the second period when Bryant all but claimed a well-merited hat-trick after his crisp half-volley flew inches wide. At last, Tottenham carved out a decent move to produce their sole riposte when Fred Barnett's fine run and cross was met by Andy Thompson to head past Lansdale.

The final word came from Millwall, however. A Tottenham corner was cleared to Alf Black, who was definitely loitering with intent. Finding himself with acres of room, Alf's acute awareness fed the speedy Jack Cock. The former England man was quick to return the ball to Black, whose fine positioning, despite being on the receiving end of a painful tackle, enabled him to secure the Lions's fifth goal of the match.

This was an exceptional and a superior performance from Millwall, who never let Spurs rest for a moment, and was a perfect revenge for the 2–1 defeat incurred at White Hart Lane earlier in the season. But the winning run ended at Middlesbrough, and between then and the end of the season the Lions were to win just two more games to finish in 14th place.

Millwall 5   Tottenham Hotspur 1
Bryant (2),   Thompson
Readman (pen),
Landells, Black

Millwall: Lansdale, Hill, Pipe, Martin, Bryant, Graham, Chance, Landells, Cock, Readman, Black.

Tottenham Hotspur: Spiers, Forster, Poynton, Lowdell, Helliwell, Smith, Barnett, Thompson, Osborne, Elkes, Dimmock.

7

CARDIFF CITY V MILLWALL

6 December 1930   **Second Division**
Ninian Park, Cardiff   **Attendance: 8,000**

The age-old adage 'you do not always get what you deserve' can apply to many things in life, and football is among them. From a Millwall perspective, the result of this match was a case in point. Coming into the game on the back of a 4–1 win over Plymouth Argyle, Millwall should really have acquired maximum points from this encounter; nonetheless, the Lions found themselves two goals down in first 10 minutes when Walter Robbins supplied the cross for Emmerson to open the scoring in the ninth minute. Emmerson reciprocated in kind 60 seconds later when he helped Robbins to register the Bluebirds' second. Early indications can be misleading, as Cardiff, who appeared to be in for a comfortable afternoon, found to their cost.

In an amazing turn of fortunes, Millwall were back on level terms 30 minutes later after serving up some exciting football. The first goal came when John Readman profited from a mix-up between Smith and Keenor to

South Wales was not a happy hunting ground for Lions goalkeeper Duncan Yuill who conceded four goals for the second time in four weeks in the Principality. The other occasion came at Vetch Field when Swansea Town beat Millwall 4–1.

reduce City's lead. Further Millwall efforts saw them gain two corners, which both resulted in goals and turned the game completely on its head. From the first corner, John Readman executed a splendid header to level the scores, while the second saw Jack Cock claim his 13th goal of the campaign to give the Lions the lead at the interval.

The normally reliable Jack Cock then fluffed an easy chance early in the second half, before Robbins made him pay with his second goal and Cardiff's equaliser in the 49th minute. After Cock had increased Millwall's lead from a Harry Wadsworth cross, the Lions continued to perform well and should have produced their second away win of the season. Unfortunately, Cock compounded his earlier lapse by missing another two gilt-edged chances after Wadsworth had set him up. Cardiff's equaliser came when Helsby's through ball found Robbins, who fired home a swerving drive that went like a bullet past Duncan Yuill to complete his hat-trick and give the Welshmen an undeserved point with one of the last kicks of the game.

Cardiff City 4   Millwall 4
Emmerson,   Readman (2), Cock (2)
Robbins (3)

Cardiff City: Evans (L), Smith, Hardy, Helsby, Keenor, Blackburn, Emmerson, Wake, Valentine, Jones, Robbins.
Millwall: Yuill, Sweetman, Pipe, Newcomb, Hancock, Graham, Wadsworth, Readman, Cock, Forsyth, Poxton.

8

BRADFORD CITY V MILLWALL

18 February 1933
Valley Parade, Bradford

Second Division
Attendance; 8,095

If medals were awarded for influence in winning the toss, then this meeting in Yorkshire would have taken gold. A severe snowstorm an hour before kick-off had an adverse effect on the attendance, despite the Bantams doing well in the League.

The weather abated somewhat at the kick-off, although Millwall did have a strong breeze behind them, but they made the most of the conditions and took an early lead. In their first serious attack down the left, the ensuing cross found City defender Sam Barkas wanting – mistiming his tackle on the Lions centre-forward George Bond. Bond's shot deceived the slow-reacting City goalkeeper, who could not prevent the ball from sneaking in at the post. City responded in kind, but Hallows could only fire his effort straight at Lions 'keeper Willie Wilson. Doubts must have been forming about whether the game could continue, as the blinding snow was having an adverse affect on City's defence.

Former bricklayer George Bond hit his second hat-trick of the season in the 5-1 demolition of Bradford City at Valley Parade.

The blizzard was still raging when the Lions scored a second goal after 13 minutes. The ball was played back to Gill, who should have gathered without any problems, but he elected to fly-kick instead, only to suffer the inevitable consequences; the hapless 'keeper thumped his attempted clearance against the onrushing Jimmy Forsyth, only for the ball to rebound into the unguarded goal.

What with the weather and two fortuitous goals for the visitors, the home support became slightly agitated. It seemed that their only hope would be abandonment. The pitch markings had been totally obliterated and the game was becoming farcical. Despite consulting a linesman, the referee allowed the game to continue, but within a minute he called a halt to proceedings.

With the storm relenting somewhat, the official wisely decided to keep fans and players waiting to see if the game could be continued. After a break of 18 minutes or so, and to the amazement of everyone, the contest resumed, with the pitch lying under a couple of inches of snow.

The enforced break may have given City a chance to save the game, but not a chance to win. They did reduce Millwall's lead, however, when Stan Alexander, who was to become a Lion the following October, scored in the 28th minute after Moore slipped a delightful square pass for Stan to thunder his drive high into Wilson's net from just outside the box.

If City had notions of a comeback, they were forgotten when Millwall registered a third goal after 32 minutes. The goal arose when Bradford defender Peachey was penalised for handball some 30 yards from goal. Skipper Len Graham sent the free-kick powerfully towards the City goal, and a slight deflection took it out of Gill's reach and into the net.

So the elements and a fair amount of good fortune saw the Lions 3–1 ahead at half-time. When it started snowing yet again, the teams forsook their half-time break to immediately change over ends – a very good idea given the inconsistency of the inclement weather.

City's problems could not only be blamed on the weather, they also faced a resolute and unyielding Millwall team, although City 'keeper Gill did manage to enjoy one fleeting moment of triumph when Bert Bloxham sent in a low, vicious cross shot, forcing Gill into a spectacular one-handed save.

The home side were shown how it should be done when George Bond scored twice in a minute. City left-back Barkas was at fault again with his decision-making when he attempted to dribble his way out of trouble; in such conditions it was pure folly and he was dispossessed by Bloxham, who steered the ball across to Bond to finish with a low drive after 64 minutes.

Bond, a bricklayer by trade, had already laid the foundations for Millwall's fourth away win of the season, and straight from the restart gained possession to run through a thoroughly dispirited City team to complete his second hat-trick of the season. This depressing defeat, City's fifth on the spin, left them in sixth place, level on points with the Lions in seventh.

Bradford City 1   Millwall 5
Alexander   Bond (3), Forsyth, Graham

Bradford City: Gill, Bicknell, Barkas, Redfern, Peachey, Bauld, Watmough, Alexander, Hallows, Peel, Moore.
Millwall: Wilson, Walsh, Pipe, Newcomb, Hancock, Graham, Bloxham, Harkins, Bond, Forsyth, Poxton.

9

MILLWALL V MANCHESTER UNITED

4 March 1933
The Den, London

Second Division
Attendance: 22,587

This was Millwall's fifth consecutive season of Second Division football, and they would go on to finish in seventh place – a record that was held for 39 years, until the 1971–72 campaign when the Lions took the third spot.

Following this victory over United, Millwall's only competitive success over the Red Devils so far, a higher position in the table may have been achieved had it not been for one distressing occurrence. It came towards the end of the month; after defeating Charlton Athletic at the Valley, the entire club went into shock when manager Bob Hunter passed away on the 29 March. Bob's association with Millwall dated back to 1897 and the team were heavily affected by his death, failing to win any of the eight remaining fixtures.

Hunter would have enjoyed this match. The tackling was hard, but clean, and the game must rank as one of the best seen at the Den during that season.

Lancastrian Bert Roberts' two goals against Manchester United gave Millwall their only competitive victory so far over the Reds.

United, as expected, were strong in approaching the penalty area, but beyond that, their penetration and finishing were weak. This was to be their downfall and the main reason why they finished up empty-handed.

United were clearly the better team until Millwall scored in the 28th minute, and from that moment on there was only going to be one winner, with United never looking likely to save the game. United's new signing, Scottish international Neil Dewar, was a constant threat, but he lacked support and was continually thwarted by Frank Hancock's close attention. The vital breakthrough came when Millwall's most productive forward, the Lancashire-born Harry Roberts, scored from close range, courtesy of Bert Bloxham's pass.

Following the slow start to the first half, the Lions flew out of traps at the beginning of the second 45 minutes and for 10 minutes pegged United back on the defence. Hoping to add to their opening goal, Millwall found the Reds 'keeper John Moody in sparkling form, as he kept out goal-bound headers from Jimmy Forsyth and George Bond.

When United did threaten, they found Millwall's former Newcastle United goalkeeper Willie Wilson a commanding presence. His handling was immense, giving great confidence to his fellow defenders. Having got the measure of United, Millwall were unfortunate not to add further goals, with the two Jimmys, Forsyth and Poxton, both coming close to scoring.

Midway through the second half, Millwall made the game safe when ex-England international Roberts notched his second goal of the match, with Bloxham again the provider.

Millwall 2   Manchester United 0
Roberts (2)

Millwall: Wilson, Walsh, Pipe, Newcomb, Hancock, Graham; Bloxham, Roberts, Bond, Forsyth, Poxton.
Manchester United: Moody, Mellor, Jones, Vincent, Frame, McLachlan, Warburton, Hine, Dewar, McDonald, Stewart.

10

MILLWALL V

LEICESTER CITY

27 January 1934   **FA Cup Fourth Round**
The Den, London   **Attendance: 34,459**

The Lions came into this tie on the back of six victories in eight matches. One of those wins came against Accrington Stanley in the third round, which set up an attractive clash against First Division opposition Leicester, who were making their first appearance at Cold Blow Lane.

The fans' hopes for a classic game were not to be disappointed, and those who witnessed the match saw a pulsating and exciting encounter that lived up to the best of English Cup football.

For those Millwall supporters looking for an upset, they were to be disappointed, as Leicester's class shone through for virtually all of the game. But the Lions had their moments, and merely taking part in this nine-goal thriller would be of some consolation.

By half-time, Leicester had an unassailable lead of four goals to one. Sep Smith put them ahead when his strike from an acute angle went in off a post. Somewhat surprisingly, Millwall found an equaliser when Laurie Fishlock's splendid cross was met by the head of George Phillips. Back came

Scot Jimmy Yardley only scored five league goals all season but took his FA Cup tally to four in two cup ties, with a double against Leicester City.

Leicester to capitalise on some poor Millwall marking, with Londoner Arthur Chandler forcing home a knock-down from Arthur Lochhead. The non-stop action saw Fishlock send in a screamer that had the crowd screaming 'Goal!', only to miss by a whisker. Millwall's Stan Alexander had a shot at goal, but only managed to thump the City crossbar.

Failing to score again during their best spell of dominance, Millwall fell further behind when Arthur Maw's volley flew into the Millwall net for goal number three. Leicester's fourth goal had a touch of controversy about it; Danny Liddle appeared to kick the ball out of Wilson's hands with one foot, before pirouetting to thump home with the other.

The second half had barely started when Leicester scored a fifth goal through Maw. There was nothing that Millwall could do but go forward, and it was Jimmy Yardley who set in motion an exciting finale when he fired home a terrific shot to reduce the arrears. But the quality of Maw and Adcock was again evident when they combined to give Lochhead the chance of obtaining number six. Despite the deficit, the crowd were still roaring the Lions on to give it one last hurrah. When Harry Roberts proffered Yardley a chance, he spurned it, much to the dismay of the crowd. The Scot made amends seconds later, however, by obtaining Millwall's third with another finely taken goal, in what was probably the most exhilarating Cup match seen at the Den since the Middlesbrough game, seven years earlier.

Millwall 3   Leicester City 6
Phillips, Yardley (2)   Smith, Chandler (2), Maw, Liddell, Lochhead

Millwall: Wilson, Walsh, Pipe, Hawkins, Turnbull, Forsyth, Alexander, Phillips, Yardley, Roberts, Fishlock.
Leicester City: McLaren, Black, Wood, Smith, Heywood, Grosvenor, Adcock, Maw, Chandler, Lochhead, Liddle.

11

MANCHESTER CITY

V MILLWALL

17 September 1938　　　　　　　**Second Division**
Maine Road, Manchester　　　　**Attendance: 27,437**

Now back in the Second Division after an absence of four years, Millwall were making their first ever excursion to Maine Road, and what a memorable visit it turned out to be. After winning their first two games of the season 5–0 and 3–0, City then contrived to lose the next three, and to concede 12 goals.

This blip necessitated some changes for the fixture against the Lions, so City brought in Jack Robinson to replace the legendary Frank Swift in goal, and new centre-half Lou Cardwell, who had been signed from Blackpool the day before. City's new boys could not have wished for a better start when Jackie Bray fastened onto a clearance from a corner to billow Harry Pearson's net in the seventh minute.

This would be the best it got for the home team. Even before the break, Millwall had two decent chances to equalise, and in another attack a Tom Brolly header inadvertently knocked the whistle out of the referee's mouth! Despite having the better of the play, City's one other effort of note came

Long Eaton born Don Barker led Millwall's recovery in the second-half by scoring two goals, which saw the Lions turn a one goal deficit at the break into a resounding 6–1 victory at Maine Road.

from Jimmy Heale, who produced an excellent save from Pearson. Any further threat to the Millwall goal was to be nipped in the bud by the excellent Eddie Chiverton and his co-defenders, who would not allow City even a sniff of another chance.

After the turnaround came the Millwall whirlwind, which may have surprised some of the assembled scribes. One reporter stated that he saw 'the writing on the wall' after the break, but even he could never have expected the torrent that the Lions would unleash, as they registered three goals in seven explosive minutes at the start of the second half. The equaliser arrived in the 53rd minute with Don Barker's rocket from outside the penalty area, before Billy Walsh capped a fine solo run and dribble to put the Lions ahead 60 seconds later.

Sid Rawlings, having given Gregg a torrid afternoon, helped himself to Millwall's next couple of goals: the first with a shot from way out after 57 minutes, before adding a fourth in the 72nd minute after Walsh opened City up with a superb pass. As Millwall continued to toy with Manchester, the game was all but up in the 77th minute when Jimmy Richardson headed goal number five following a corner.

After City conceded the fifth, a flag seen fluttering above the grandstand beforehand was lowered to half-mast by an irate City fan. Protocol was restored when the flag was hoisted to its rightful place shortly afterwards. This event coincided with Millwall celebrating a sixth goal, thanks to Barker; to complete the scoring, and seal Manchester City's capitulation and humiliation three minutes from time.

So Millwall recorded their first away victory of the campaign – against a side who had been Football League Champions in 1937 and were to suffer relegation a year later, despite being the highest scorers in the First Division. City, however, did manage to rally to finish fifth, eight places above Millwall in 13th place.

Manchester City 1   Millwall 6
Bray   Barker (2), Walsh, Rawlings (2), Richardson

Manchester City: Robinson, Clark, Gregg, McDowell, Cardwell, Bray, Dunkley, Herd, Howe, Heale, Brook.

Millwall: Pearson, Smith E., Inns, Brolly, Chiverton, Forsyth, Rawlings, Richardson, Walsh, Barker, Smith J.R.

12

WALSALL V

MILLWALL

13 November 1948 **Third Division South**
Fellows Park, Walsall **Attendance: 9,604**

This extraordinary meeting produced Millwall's highest aggregate score in the Football League. With the rain falling heavily, fans may have been put off, but those who did attend were in for an amazing spectacle.

Millwall were first to attack, with some long passing movements in which Lions' leading goalscorer, Jimmy Constantine, was prominent. This was a distinct source of worry to Walsall, with one header just clearing the crossbar. Both sides had difficulty in controlling the greasy ball, but Walsall seemed to manage better; a skillful touch from Phil Chapman providing Johnny Devlin with an opportunity that he failed to take. In another attack, Devlin managed a header, although it was defended comfortably by Malcolm Finlayson.

Walsall had the wind taken out of their sails in the 16th minute when Millwall suddenly burst into action, with outside-right Johnny Johnson firing in a fierce cross shot that home 'keeper Jack Lewis could only push into the path of Ronnie Mansfield, who gleefully slotted home. Straight from the restart, Devlin found himself on a one-to-one with Finlayson, whose bravery in diving at his fellow Scot's feet saw him carried off with an injury.

Millwall made the necessary amendments to the side, which saw Constantine don the goalkeeper's jersey, with Mansfield moving into the centre and coming close to extending the Lions' lead with a hard drive. But it was Walsall who scored next, when Jimmy Conde equalised after Albert Mullard started the move in the 28th minute. Barely 60 seconds had lapsed before the Saddlers went in front after Chapman netted with a glorious header, thanks to Devlin's ingenuity. Constantine then showed his worth when he diverted Mullard's effort from a corner to stop the Lions from falling further behind just before the break. The second half resumed with Millwall still down to 10 men. Walsall had to make some changes, with the injured full-back Norman Male filling in at outside-left. It was, surprisingly, the limping Male who put the Saddlers 3–1 up after hobbling into the area to finish off another Devlin assist.

A welcome sight for Millwall was the return of Malcolm Finlayson, who was sporting a heavy plaster above his right eye. His appearance certainly revitalised his teammates; they went straight back to the other end to score a second when Johnny Short despatched a magnificent drive low into the corner of the net. Now back at full strength, Millwall began to dictate the proceedings. Lewis brought off a spectacular save from Willie Hurrell, but the 'keeper was a mere spectator when Mansfield struck the woodwork with a terrific drive.

Unbelievably, and in the space of three incredible minutes, the Lions were in front once more, drawing level after 67 minutes when Short scored his second and Millwall's third, before Hurrell, to everyone's amazement, put them ahead. The lead, however, was short-lived, as Male restored parity in the 71st minute to make it 4–4 after Finlayson fumbled Chapman's original effort. The thrills and spills continued unabated, with no one daring to predict the outcome. Millwall's Tom Brolly thought that he may have notched the winner when scoring directly from a free-kick with seven minutes to go, but the Saddlers, not to be denied, hit back immediately when Chapman made 5–5 after nipping in between two Lions defenders in the 86th minute. By this time the crowd were delirious – it must have been one of the most bizarre matches the Lions had ever appeared in. The sting in the tail came with three minutes left, and it was Millwall who managed to tip the scales in their favour. In a last throw of dice, the ball reached John Short, who bulleted a spectacular shot from 25 yards that rippled the back of the Walsall net for the genial Geordie's first ever League hat-trick in a truly wondrous 6–5 victory.

So ended a remarkable game, where credit must be afforded to the commitment of all 22 players, who produced a splendid feast of skillful football in very difficult conditions. It was a shame that the first Fellows Park attendance of the season to drop below 10,000 were the only witnesses to a little piece of footballing history.

These few lines from Lewis Carroll sum up Millwall's day in Wonderland: 'And thick and fast they came at last. And more, and more, and more.'

Walsall 5	Millwall 6
Condie, Chapman (2),	Mansfield, Short (3),
Male (2)	Hurrell, Brolly

Walsall: Lewis, Methley, Male, Walters, Foulkes, Newman, Aldred, Mullard, Chapman, Devlin, Condie.
Millwall: Finlayson, Fisher G., Tyler, Reeves, Simmonds, Brolly, Johnson, Hurrell, Constantine, Short, Mansfield.

13

BRISTOL ROVERS V MILLWALL

24 January 1953   **Third Division South**
Eastville, Bristol   **Attendance: 31,035**

In the general scheme of things, a point against the champions elect is nothing to be sniffed at, especially as this was the first point that Rovers had dropped at home since 27 September. But the undoubted hero for Bristol was their goalkeeper, Bert Hoyle, who clambered out of his sickbed and went on to give an exceptional and courageous performance.

Millwall had beaten Rovers 3–0 at the Den back in September, but both clubs had progressed to such an extent that by the time of the return game, Rovers were leading the pack at the top of the table, with the Lions following nicely in the slipstream in fourth place.

A draw was a fitting result for the most exciting and satisfying game of the season at Eastville. The gates were closed prior to kick-off and an expectant full house witnessed an exhibition worthy of the occasion. The game was played in a wonderful spirit by two sets of highly disciplined players who did not allow the atmosphere to affect them.

Alan Monkhouse the Lions goalscorer at Bristol Rovers, characterized here by Syd Jordan, whose drawings of the Millwall players regularly appeared in the Kentish Mercury.

The game at Eastville attracted nearly 31,000 spectators who saw the Rovers take the lead through Geoff Bradford with Lions Gerry Bowler and George Fisher unable to prevent the score.

CROSSING-THE-LINE CEREMONY — Bradford, on one knee, alongside goalkeeper Finlayson, scores Bristol Rovers' goal at Eastville. Left is Bowler. Fisher is on the goal-line, and Petherbridge by the goalpost.

It was Rovers who opened the scoring in the fifth minute, when centre-forward Vic Lambden scooted out to right wing to take John McIvenny's pass. Lambden then made a perfect pass, which caught the Millwall defence on the wrong foot. This allowed George Petherbridge to get the better of right-back Alex Jardine and find Geoff Bradford, who followed up to score from an impossible angle for his 20th goal of the season.

The Millwall equaliser in the 21st minute came when Rovers defender Harry Bamford was pulled up for handball. The free-kick enabled both Johnny Johnson and Johnny Short to surge deep into the Bristol half. When the cross came over, it was met by outside-left Alan Monkhouse, who timed his run to perfection to place a deft header out of Hoyle's reach and into the net at the far post.

Despite the defences dominating, errors were made that offered opportunities to both attacks. But Rovers had the better of the first half, nearly regaining the lead when Bradford's header from the edge of the penalty area hit the Millwall crossbar.

LAMBDEN (Rovers), Fisher and Finlayson (Millwall), all on the ground, as Referee Mr F. an infringement.

Bill Roost had a late chance to give Rovers victory, but Millwall were not without some telling moments. The

This goalmouth tussle ended when Millwall were awarded a free-kick, much to the relief of George Fisher and goalkeeper Malcolm Finlayson.

Lions nearly ended Bristol's unbeaten home run when new signing from Sheffield United, Freddy Smith, was denied a debut goal after narrowly missing, and later his full-blooded drive was foiled by Hoyle's excellent stop.

So Millwall, slightly better in attack, came close to achieving an impressive double, but were more than happy to claim a draw from a scintillating match. Rovers went on to claim the Third Division South title with 64 points, while the Lions would frustratingly finish in the runner-up spot on 62 points, no doubt rueing the home defeat by Norwich City, their only home loss after Christmas.

Match official Mr Read summed up the match: 'It was a real pleasure to referee such a fine match. I enjoyed every minute of it.'

Bristol Rovers 1   Millwall 1
Bradford   Monkhouse

Bristol Rovers: Hoyle, Bamford, Fox, Pitt, Warren, Sampson, McIlvenny, Roost, Lambden, Bradford, Petherbridge.
Millwall: Finlayson, Jardine, Fisher G., Short, Bowler, Saward, Johnson, Smith F., Shepherd, Morgan, Monkhouse.

14

MILLWALL V
TORQUAY UNITED

12 January 1957   **Third Division South**
The Den, London   **Attendance: 12,574**

The third-round FA Cup victory over Crystal Palace the week before gave Millwall the mouth-watering prospect of facing Newcastle United in the next round at the Den. The publicity surrounding the Newcastle tie could have sidetracked the team, who could have been forgiven if their thoughts had been elsewhere when they entertained high-flying Torquay. But one strategic move made by manager Ron Gray for Torquay's visit was to push the granite-hard right-back Stan Anslow up to lead the attack alongside Johnny Shepherd. The move proved to be inspirational, as Millwall achieved vengeance over second-place Torquay for the 7–2 mauling handed out back in September.

For the first 15 minutes Torquay certainly lived up to their top billing and went ahead after just five minutes when United skipper Dennis Lewis's free-kick found Sam Collins to lob the ball into the net. The visitors nearly went two up within minutes when the unmarked Ron Shaw blasted a left-foot drive that Lloyd managed to push away to safety.

MILLWALL
FOOTBALL CLUB

Founded
~1885

v.

Saturday, January 12th, 1957   TORQUAY

DIRECTORS

Chairman: F. C. PURSER, Esq.
Vice-Chairman: H. E. HOWARD, Esq.

T. CAYGILL, Esq.   S. C. EDGE, Esq.   DR. D. EPPEL
G. S. KENURE, Esq.   J. P. WATSON, Esq., C.B.E., M.I.M.E.
N. WEEDON, Esq.

Hon. Medical Officers: DR. D. EPPEL   DR. J. A. HENRY
Secretary: CECIL F. LINNEY   Team Manager: RON GRAY
Trainer-Coach: J. D. SHORT

Registered Office: THE DEN, NEW CROSS, S.E.14   Phone: NEWcross 2700

Official Programme   **4**d   The right of admission to grounds
is reserved.

Stan Anslow, normally a full-back certainly hit the goal-trail when appearing as a makeshift centre-forward. He was one of two Millwall players' to register hat-tricks in the thumping of Torquay United.

Millwall's only effort in this spell came from the boot of captain Colin Rawson's stinging 25-yard shot from George Hazlett's centre, which was competently held by Mervyn Gill in the Torquay goal. The foothold that Millwall needed to get back into the game materialised in the 12th minute when Hazlett's cross was intercepted by United's right-back John Smith, but Smith's intended header back to the advancing Gill carried too much height and left the 'keeper stranded as the ball nestled in the back of the net.

This stroke of luck got the Lions going and certainly affected Torquay, who were clearly rattled. One nasty challenge appeared to confirm this, with centre-forward Ted Calland's foul on Lloyd earning Calland a severe talking-to from the referee. The assault raised the Lions' hackles and, back in the picture, they stormed forward, forcing the Torquay defence into hurried clearances.

Millwall went deservedly in front when a slick move down the right wing and from Hazlett's cross, Shepherd from close range made it 2–1 in the 25th minute. Torquay hit back with some strong attacks, but these were confidently dealt with by Lloyd's calming assurance. The Lions should have stretched their lead further just before the interval, when George Veitch's long throw caught out the Torquay reararguard to find Gordon Pulley, but Pulley's lack of composure saw him fire the effort wide.

Not for the first time in their history, Millwall hit the ground running at the start of the second half with three goals in seven minutes. Stan Anslow

Johnny Shepherd was also a contender for claiming ownership of the match ball with his treble against the Gulls.

got the ball rolling in the 48th minute when he wrong-footed Gill to toe poke Alex Jardine's free-kick following Lewis's transgression for handball. Four minutes later, Anslow justified his position in attack by working with Shepherd by thumping home the fourth goal.

The Anslow and Shepherd partnership was at it again as they split the visitors' defence open in the 55th minute. This time, Anslow was the provider for Shepherd to turn the ball past Gill for the fifth. Torquay's earlier poise had been shot to pieces, and in the 65th minute Shepherd continued the rout to claim his hat-trick when his well-judged lob found an empty net. Defensively the Gulls were in total disarray, but their forwards continued to play some decent football and were duly rewarded after 72 minutes; Shaw was fouled in the area by Ray Brand and it was left to Sam Collins to fire home the penalty for his second goal.

But Millwall were in no mood to stop at six, as they prolonged Torquay's discomfort with some speedy and accurate football. Another excellent move left the Gulls' defence all over the shop, which resulted in a suicidal back pass that failed to reach Gill. Anslow's instinct was not that of a full-back, but of a goal-poacher supreme, as he joyfully found the net to complete his hat-trick. Millwall continued to dominate for the rest of the game, while a shell-shocked Torquay team were only grateful not concede any more goals.

Millwall 7	Torquay United 2
Smith J.V. (og),	Collins S. (2, 1 pen)
Shepherd (3),	
Anslow (3)	

Millwall: Lloyd, Jardine, Smith J., Veitch, Brand, Rawson, Hazlett, Shepherd, Anslow, Summersby, Pulley.
Torquay United: Gill, Smith J.V., Smith H., Lewis, Norman, James, Shaw, Collins S., Calland, Mills, Collins A.

15

MILLWALL V

PORT VALE

13 December 1958   **Fourth Division**
The Den, London   **Attendance: 10,390**

Millwall faced a stiff examination of their character following their shock dismissal by non-League Worcester City from the FA Cup the previous Saturday. What better test then, but to face Fourth Division leaders Port Vale in a top-of-the-table clash? Overnight rain had continued into the Saturday morning of the game, making the Den's surface a bit of a mudbath, but entirely playable.

It was an excellent start to the match as both sides showed their intentions very early on, and this was to continue throughout in a hard-fought contest.

In the visitors' first serious attack they came close to opening the scoring, but were foiled by Lions 'keeper Reg Davies, who grabbed the ball just before Vale debut-maker Graham Barnett was about to pounce. Davies was again called into action when he dealt with Brian Jackson's wicked cross-shot with admirable style.

Both teams were moving the ball exceptionally well, despite the muddy conditions, and, with Vale on top at this stage, the Valiants were awarded a

The cover of the match programme for Millwall's epic encounter with champions elect Port Vale at The Den.

free-kick on the edge of the Millwall area for a foul on Jack Cunliffe. The Port Vale man took the kick himself, which was headed clear. The Lions were showing no hangover from the Worcester disgrace and nearly took the lead when Hutton's hard-driven shot seemed to be heading for the bottom corner of the net, until Roy Pritchard cleared off the line.

Port Vale's response was a menacing break at pace, and when Cunliffe took Barnett's long through ball, he could only fire his effort wide of the Millwall goal. Joey Broadfoot then livened up proceedings when he stung the hands of Vale's other debutant, goalkeeper Ken Hancock, who took two attempts to save. Another dangerous Vale move was brought to a sudden end when the eager Barnett was pulled up for offside.

Play evened up in the last 10 minutes, but Port Vale went close when Jackson's effort skimmed the crossbar. Millwall hit back after Heckman got clean through, only to be denied by Hancock's block. The conditions seemed to have no effect on the contest as play was flowing from end to end; however, Davies had to be alert to save Steele's excellent header.

All this attacking enterprise certainly merited a goal, and eventually one came for Millwall. A corner taken by Broadfoot on the right was cleared to a distance of around 25 yards, where Lions skipper Colin Rawson was ideally placed to return it into the bottom corner of net, giving Hancock no chance. The visitors stormed back with a vengeance, only to fall further behind six minutes later. A mistake in the Vale half saw Joe Hutton pounce on Albert Leake's miskick, leaving the diminutive Scot to run on and beat Hancock for goal number two.

Port Vale showed why they were topping the table with some very speedy and decisive attacks, in which Davies saved another good header, this time from Barnett. The visitors had a chance to reduce Millwall's lead when Harry Poole returned Davies's under-hit goal-kick harmlessly back over the bar. But Millwall went close to scoring again after Hutton found Alec Moyse, whose near miss was the last action of the half.

Port Vale's attacking threat had brought them no reward in the first half, but their efforts were to bear fruit in the opening 15 minutes of the second half. An excellent run from Poole forced a corner that caused a scramble in the Lions' goalmouth, from which Steele headed home in the 53rd minute. They were level on the hour when a mistake in the Millwall defence gave Barnett the chance to force the ball in at the second attempt.

Boosted and full of confidence, Vale kept the Millwall defence on their toes, but Davies was again the saviour when he got the better of Poole. At the other end, Hancock stopped a Broadfoot effort, whose run had left three Vale defenders in his wake. Alan Crowshaw then tested the young Vale 'keeper with a thunderbolt effort. Millwall got lucky when Davies instinctively stuck out a foot to stop Barnett's fierce drive, and moments later Cunliffe fared no better with his attempt. The game was finely balanced and the outcome could go either way – the team scoring next would surely take the spoils.

As Millwall pressed for a winner, Heckman again brought out the best in Hancock, who made a stunning save with 10 minutes to go. Having kept Vale on the back foot for the last 15 minutes or so, Millwall's patience paid off with the award of a penalty-kick when the bubbly Hutton was flattened in the box. The onus to take the spot-kick was on Irish left-back Pat Brady and he did not disappoint, dispatching his shot beyond Hancock to put Millwall back into the lead in the 83rd minute. An excellent match was finally decided after Broadfoot's tidy cross was converted from close range by the inspired Hutton.

When the inaugural Fourth Division season was completed, Millwall eventually finished in a disappointing ninth place, mainly due to drawing too many games, while Port Vale claimed the title and in 46 games scored an amazing 110 goals, five of which came in the return game at Vale Park when beating Millwall 5–2.

Millwall 4	Port Vale 2
Rawson, Hutton (2),	Steele, Barnett
Brady R. (pen)	

Millwall: Davies, Redmond, Brady R., Humphries, Harper, Rawson, Broadfoot, Hutton, Moyse, Heckman, Crowshaw.

Port Vale: Hancock, Raine, Pritchard, Kinsey, Leake, Miles, Jackson, Steele, Poole, Barnett, Cunliffe.

16

MILLWALL V CHESTER

23 April 1960
The Den, London

Fourth Division
Attendance: 9,647

Millwall's penultimate game of the season saw their chance for the fourth automatic promotion place hanging by a thread. But with just one more fixture to fulfil, at Southport, the hopes of a higher grade of football lay firmly with the Lions' rivals dropping points. Those teams had games in hand, however, which left Millwall needing snookers.

For over an hour it appeared that Millwall had already given up the dream of Third Division football and were simply looking forward to the summer break, especially after Alf Ackerman contrived to miss two sitters. The Lions seemed content to let the game drift aimlessly towards half-time while holding a one-goal lead. The goal came in the 23rd minute after a saunter down the left by Dave Smith, the Gloucestershire cricketer. His centre was met by centre-forward Barry Pierce, who collected his 16th goal of the season.

The visitors' best chance came just after the break, when Chester's Ron Davies lobbed his namesake, Millwall goalkeeper Reg Davies, only for the

The right of admission to grounds is reserved

MILLWALL
FOOTBALL CLUB
Founded ~1885

Saturday, April 23rd, 1960

To-day's Match v.

Chester

Football League, Div. 4   Kick-off 3.15 p.m.

Next Saturday, April 30th, 1960

Tooting & Mitcham v. Bromley

London Senior Cup Final   Kick-off 3 p.m.

DIRECTORS :

Chairman: F. C. PURSER, Esq.

Vice-Chairman: G. S. KENURE, Esq.

T. CAYGILL, Esq.   S. C. EDGE, Esq.   Dr. D EPPEL.
N. WEEDON, Esq.   J. M. SEED, Esq.

Hon. Medical Officers: Dr. D. EPPEL.   Dr. J. A. HENRY.

Secretary: D. G. BORLAND.   Manager: J. R. SMITH.

Assistant Manager: RON GRAY.   Trainer-Coach: J. D. SHORT.

Registered Office : THE DEN, NEW CROSS. S.E.14.   Phone : NEW Cross 3143/4

OFFICIAL PROGRAMME 4 D.

Outside-left Dave Smith scored his only goal for Millwall in the 7-1 trouncing of Chester. He was also played cricket for Gloucestershire and England.

ball to bounce wide of the target. The sound of slow handclapping began, accompanied by pockets of isolated booing around the ground when news filtered through to the players that promotion rivals Watford were winning. It was just the impetus that Millwall required to raise their game. But then came a gift from the gods: a very contentious penalty was awarded to Millwall, and it was to lead an unprecedented goal glut, with a further half a dozen goals arriving in the last 24 minutes.

The penalty controversy arose when Chester defender George Spruce struggled to control a bouncing ball in the penalty area, with the crowd yelling 'Handball!' The unsighted referee, Mr Carr, concurred, bringing the regulatory torrent of protests from Spruce's teammates, two of whom were booked.

Liverpool born Barry Pierce scored his 16th and 17th goals of the season in the unlikely rout of Chester at Cold Blow Lane.

Left-back Pat Brady began the deluge when converting the spot-kick in the 67th minute. The Lions built on this stroke of luck to push forward with confidence, searching for more booty. Bumpstead, Ackerman and Pierce began to penetrate and exploit a sorry-looking Chester defence. The funnel system that Millwall had been operating over the course of the season went into overdrive on this occasion.

The marauding Bumpstead put it on a plate for Ackerman to slam home the third goal after 70 minutes. Six minutes later, outside-right Joe Broadfoot was the creator for Pierce to round former Welsh international goalkeeper Ron Howells and grab the fourth. The luckless Spruce then sliced Smith's tantalising cross past Howells for goal number five in the 77th minute. Chester's lonely riposte came five minutes from time when Alec Croft's effort cannoned off centre-half Ray Brand for the game's second own-goal.

Millwall were far from finished, and a minute later Dave Smith's delightful weaving run down the byline ended when he nonchalantly flicked home the sixth. The goal-fest was concluded by the superb Dave Harper, when he fired home the seventh with one of the last kicks of the game.

Despite this frolic in the spring sunshine, Millwall lost out on the promotion prize and would have to face another two seasons of basement football before reaching their goal in 1962.

Millwall 7	Chester 1
Pierce (2),	Brand (og)
Brady P (pen),	
Ackerman, Smith D.,	
Harper, Spruce (og)	

Millwall: Davies R.W., Redmond, Brady P., Harper, Brand, Howells J., Broadfoot, Ackerman, Pierce, Bumpstead, Smith.
Chester: Howells R., Hughes, Gill, Jones, Spruce, Clempson, Cooper, Kelly, Davies R.T., Pimlott, Croft.

17

MILLWALL V

YORK CITY

17 December 1960
The Den, London

Fourth Division
Attendance; 6,706

York City were one of four clubs to gain promotion in the initial season of the new Fourth Division, but having sampled the delights of a single season in the Third Division, found themselves back in the lower tier. Before this game the Lions had already hit 50 goals in the League, but more of a concern were the 46 goals they had let in, which was slightly over two goals per game.

So goals were to be expected in this encounter against York, who had already beaten the Lions 3–2 in an opening-day fixture. From the off, Millwall went after York, and would hold territorial advantage for virtually the whole of the 90 minutes. But such advantage counts for nothing if it cannot be turned into something tangible, and it often happens that the team under the cosh break away and score.

So after pounding City in the opening phase, Millwall fell behind after 12 minutes. The goal's validity was questioned when York striker Norman Wilkinson received the ball some 30 yards from goal. With the Millwall

South African Alf Ackerman brought the Lions level with a simple tap in to make 2–2.

defence cast adrift, the referee awaited his linesman's indication regarding offside, but when none was forthcoming, he allowed Wilkinson to proceed and beat the advancing Reg Davies.

Needless to say, the official, Mr Eric Jennings, and his assistant were on the receiving end of the fans' derision. Millwall upped the huffing and puffing, but found the York defence in resolute form, and centre-half Ken Boyes was to become an outstanding figure.

A Millwall goal looked likely when leading goalscorer Peter Burridge raced down the middle, but his shot struck goalkeeper Tommy Forgan on the chest, leaving right-back George Howe to complete the clearance. Centre-forward Alf Ackerman then tried to find Burridge, but Forgan's fine anticipation ended the move.

With half-time approaching, Millwall were still finding a rock-like York defence hard to crack, with Ackerman decidedly coming off second-best in his duels with Boyes. A golden opportunity presented itself to Millwall's South African centre-forward after receiving Joe Broadfoot's low cross four yards from goal, but just as he prepared to shoot, Alf was denied by Walt Bingley's finely timed tackle.

City commenced the second half with some threatening raids, but winger Billy Hughes terminated one good opening when he carelessly ran the ball out of play. Another York move fizzled out when Colin Addison's pass was intercepted by Dennis Jackson to prevent further danger. York nearly scored again when a Millwall corner was cleared, and City quickly sprung into attack with Wilkinson in the vanguard. Ably supported by

Addison and Hughes, it was this fine interplay that set up Johnny Edgar, whose effort was deflected for a corner.

As play fluctuated, a sustained spell of Millwall pressure saw York 'keeper Forgan snuff out one threat by claiming a high cross, but moments later he was thankful to see Bingley clear the danger from yet another corner. Some nifty footwork from the balding Wilkinson bemused Lions skipper Dave Bumpstead and set up outside-left Jimmy Weir, who, to Wilkinson's chagrin, lost possession. Addison's probing foray deep into Millwall territory saw him take on and beat two opponents and unleash a rising drive that just cleared Davies's crossbar.

As Millwall's attacks continued to flounder and frustrate in equal measure, at the other end York had another two efforts flash across the Lions' penalty area, with no one being able to apply the finishing touch. A second City goal looked on the cards, but Davies denied them with a superb one-handed save from Edgar at the expense of a corner. Despite all their non-stop blustering, Millwall were caught cold with 20 minutes to go. A hard cross from Hughes found its way past a body of players, except the

lurking Wilkinson, who fired the ball back into the far side of the net.

It was all uphill for Millwall now, as all their efforts had fallen on stony ground. With nothing to lose, Millwall went all out on the attack, and leading the charge in support of the forwards were the two wing-halves, Dave Bumpstead and Alan Anderson. It was this pair who came very close to reducing York's advantage, with shots going

Leading goalscorer Peter Burridge got Millwall back into contention with his 19th goal of the season.

Alan Spears was ideally placed to grab the winner in the remarkable comeback against York City.

narrowly wide. Then a ray of hope came when the Lions finally scored in the 79th minute. It appeared to be no more than a consolation, but the wily old fox Ackerman for once got the better of Bingley. Looking up, Alf spotted the expectant Burridge, who was on hand to force home his 19th League goal of the season.

After looking so assured for nine tenths of the game, the alarm bells began to ring for City. The fans picked up on this to begin an encouraging roar, and four minutes later Millwall scored a deserved equaliser. For the first time in the game the faultless Forgan erred when challenged by Burridge, conveniently dropping the ball to allow the rejuvenated Ackerman to tap home. Alf was now finding that extra bit of pace, and it was the veteran who set up the winning goal. Outside-left Alan Spears, who had hardly seen the ball all afternoon, took up a position in the York area, and his gamble paid off when he snatched a late winner for Millwall to complete a remarkable comeback.

In a campaign in which both Millwall and York City were again prominent in the promotion stakes, however, they were unfortunately condemned to narrowly miss out on promotion. Millwall would end up in sixth spot, one place and one point behind the Minstermen.

Millwall 3   York City 2
Burridge, Ackerman,   Wilkinson (2)
Spears

Millwall: Davies, Jackson, Brady P., Bumpstead, Harper, Anderson A., Broadfoot, Jones, Ackerman, Burridge, Spears.
York City: Forgan, Bingley, Howe, Woods, Boyes, Fountain, Hughes, Addison, Wilkinson, Edgar, Weir.

18

MILLWALL V

PORT VALE

27 August 1962   **Third Division**
The Den, London   **Attendance: 20,533**

After freeing themselves of basement football, Millwall were back in the Third Division after taking the Fourth Division title the previous April. They made an excellent start to the new campaign by obtaining good draws when sharing four goals at Bristol City and a 1–1 at Port Vale, before thumping Watford 6–0 in their first home fixture.

When Port Vale last visited the Den in December 1958, the spectators were treated to six goals in a splendid game played in trying conditions. Although this game remained goalless, it was no less exciting than its predecessor. The game started at a breakneck pace that was remarkably maintained throughout the 90 minutes. The biggest crowd of the season at the Den watched the sort of game that supporters dream of. If Millwall could keep their early-season momentum on track, the players could look forward to receiving many more £5 crowd-bonus payments.

The thrill-a-minute display started when Millwall set the trend of near misses and lost chances when centre-forward Pat Terry lobbed the ball into the terraces after six minutes, despite the fact that it looked easier to find the net. Shortly afterwards, the Lions striker did likewise with a header. Not wanting to miss out on the fun, Vale followed suit in the 13th minute with the miss of the match, when Harry Poole smacked Colin Grainger's centre against the crossbar with no opponent in sight.

But the real excitement and drama was to come in the second half, as Millwall sent in wave after wave of attacks that failed to penetrate an excellently marshalled Port Vale defence. The Lions were cheered on with typical Old Kent Road fervour, which created such an atmosphere that referee Jim Finney remarked that it was an ambience that he had not even experienced in last May's Cup Final. The match official would also have a painful memory to take home with him, however. During the course of the game a pass from Saturday's hat-trick hero, Jim Towers, accidentally felled him; Jim had meant the ball to go to his wing-partner, Terry McQuade. Fortunately, the referee was able to continue after receiving treatment from the Millwall trainer.

The crowd might have seen a goal had a player put a foot on the ball, but in such a frenzied melting pot of a game, no participant seemed willing to risk being caught in possession. The intensity increased, as did the total of misses, as both sides seemed happy enough to keep up the frenetic pace. The latest culprit was Vale's striker Bert Llewellyn, who was culpable of placing his header into the waiting arms of Millwall 'keeper Reg Davies from two yards.

Pat Terry then completed an unwanted hat-trick of sorts when he rolled his effort wide of a yawning goal. Having had no luck from close quarters, Millwall altered their approach towards the end of the game by raining in shots from varying distances and from all angles. It was efforts from Terry, Towers and Dave Jones that came closest to breaking the deadlock, but Vale, with the impressive Ken Hancock in goal, held out for a point in a pulsating encounter.

Millwall 0   Port Vale 0

Millwall: Davies, Gilchrist, Brady P., Obeney, Brady R., Wilson, Broadfoot, Jones D., Terry, Towers, McQuade.

Port Vale: Hancock, Lowe, Sproson, Ford, Nicholson, Miles, Rowland, Poole, Llewellyn, Steele, Grainger.

19

MILLWALL V

BARNSLEY

13 April 1964
The Den, London

Third Division
Attendance: 11,503

With both clubs deep in the relegation mire, and following their differing fortunes over the weekend, this was a must-win game for the Lions. The Tykes were fresh from their 2–1 success at Division Two-bound Crystal Palace, while the Lions entered the fray on the back of a 1–0 loss at fellow strugglers Crewe Alexandra.

Millwall's expectation of victory brought a fraught and tense atmosphere to the Den that could be cut with a knife. The ensuing game would turn on some contentious refereeing decisions, but the upshot saw Millwall obtain two vital points and leave Barnsley the victims of a great injustice.

In the first half Barnsley had appeared to be well in control, buoyed, no doubt, by their success at Selhurst Park, and seemed to be on their way to a second South East London victory in little over 48 hours. They were given a helping hand by Millwall goalkeeper Alex Stepney, whose fumble led to Tony Leighton scoring in the eighth minute.

The illustrated cover of the Millwall v Barnsley match programme, which shows the Lower Pool of the River Thames stretching down towards Millwall's spiritual home, the Isle of Dogs.

Player-manager Billy Gray inspired his Millwall team to victory in a dramatic and a highly contentious relegation battle against Barnsley in 1964.

Leighton nearly made it two when his low drive in the 25th minute beat Stepney but swerved just wide of the post. The first whiff of controversy came when Millwall equalised for the first time after 37 minutes, with Pat Terry netting from a suspiciously offside-looking position.

Barnsley regained the lead with some composed football in the 42nd minute when Leighton won the race with Lions centre-half Bryan Snowdon to George Kerr's superb through ball to finish with cool assurance. But with the fans enjoying a half-time cup of tea, no one had any idea of what was to unfurl before their eyes in an intriguing and eventful second half.

Leading 2–1 at the break, the Yorkshiremen had kept Millwall at bay with relative ease. Then in the 56th minute, the official, Mr Geoff Roper, awarded the Lions a free-kick when Barnsley's Bobby Wood nudged Gary Townend when going for a high cross. After indicating an indirect kick some eight yards to the right of the goal, Roper then inexplicably changed his mind and awarded a penalty-kick.

Mayhem then broke out as the Barnsley players surrounded the referee, protesting with vehement indignation, but despite their protestations, Mr Roper was not going change his mind again. Over two minutes had elapsed before order was restored. It was left to Lions player-manager Billy Gray to draw the teams level from the penalty spot.

Five minutes later the Tykes blew another gasket when Millwall right-back Johnny Gilchrist drilled home a low shot to put the Lions ahead.

Claiming that their goalkeeper, Alan Hill, had been held back in his attempt to save, they again vented their spleen at an unmoved referee who allowed the goal to stand.

In those defining five minutes, Barnsley lost their shape and self-control, and centre-half Eric Winstanley became their fourth player to be booked after clattering into Millwall's Barnsley-born outside-right, Roy Senior. The match was finally settled in the 81st minute when Townend burst through a crestfallen and totally disillusioned Tykes defence to snatch the fourth goal.

Following the final whistle in a match of high intensity, the indignant Barnsley players mockingly applauded Mr Roper off the pitch. With feelings running high, the official wisely locked the door of his dressing room until tempers cooled. Even the Millwall players later admitted, 'the penalty decision was extremely harsh'.

After the dust had finally settled at the conclusion of the season, the table showed that Barnsley had survived the drop by a point, while Millwall went down with 38 points.

Millwall 4   Barnsley 2
Terry, Gray (pen),   Leighton (2)
Gilchrist, Townend.

Millwall: Stepney, Gilchrist, John, Anderson D., Snowdon, Wilson, Senior, Whitehouse, Terry, Townend, Gray.
Barnsley: Hill, Hopper, Brookes, Wood, Winstanley, Houghton, Earnshaw, Kerr, Leighton, Byrne, O'Hara.

20

MILLWALL V MIDDLESBROUGH

18 October 1965
The Den, London

Football League Cup
Third Replay
Attendance: 12,888

Having obtained a decent, if fortunate goalless draw at Ayresome Park in the first game, Millwall could now improve their standing by defeating Second Division Middlesbrough, and also measure their improvement as a club since relegation 18 months previously.

Following on from a gruelling 1–0 victory over fellow promotion contenders Swindon Town on the Saturday, Millwall would now face another full-blooded and stamina-sapping match that would require extra-time to find a winner.

This replay would have been academic had Middlesbrough's Jim Irvine not blasted his 80th-minute penalty-kick wide of Alex Stepney's goal up on Teesside, but the scene was set for the Lions and their supporters to up the tempo and the volume of noise. The game set off at a cracking pace, with a 15-minute burst of high-powered football and the usual 100 per cent effort from Billy Gray's team.

One of Millwall's finest post-war goalkeepers, Alex Stepney, seemed to improve with every game and against Middlesbrough his coolness under pressure is admirably demonstrated here with an excellent clearance.

Millwall took the lead in the eighth minute when midfielder Kenny Jones took Mickey Brown's throw-in and, without breaking his stride, sent his low drive rocketing past Eddie Connachan's dive. Millwall's breakneck start could not be sustained indefinitely, and gradually, Middlesbrough, through the prompting of Ian Gibson, started to make some headway during the latter part of the first half.

Missing their regular centre-back pairing of Brian Snowdon and Tommy Wilson, Millwall had given a debut to 16-year-old apprentice John Richardson, the manager's nephew, who formed an effective barrier with centre-half Johnny Gilchrist to force the visitors into long-range shooting. With the match entering its dying minutes, Jones's early strike appeared to

John Richardson, manager Billy Gray's nephew, made his first team debut against Middlesbrough in a League Cup replay at The Den aged 16 years and 255 days.

be enough for victory. Middlesbrough had been a persistent opponent, however, and their labour was duly rewarded to draw level after 78 minutes when Gibson's effort looped over Stepney to drop under the crossbar.

An extra 30 minutes was now required and would surely test the Lions' resolve and fitness levels, and if anyone was in doubt about these attributes, they were soon to be eating humble pie. It was outside-left Billy Neil who restored Millwall's lead in the 98th minute, when Richardson started the move that sent Barry Rowan haring down the right and crossing for Neil to emulate Jones's earlier goal with another stunning strike.

Middlesbrough wilted after this, although a Billy Horner header was cleared off the line, and they were eventually put out of their misery a minute from time. Mickey Brown sent over another telling cross for Lennie Julians to bury his header for the third goal and send a buoyant crowd home happy.

Millwall 3   Middlesbrough 1
Jones K., Neil,   Gibson
Julians

(After extra-time. Score at 90 minutes 1–1)

Millwall: Stepney, John, Cripps, Jones K., Gilchrist, Richardson, Rowan, Julians, Brown M., Jacks, Neil.
Middlesbrough: Connachan, Gates, Jones G., Horner, Rooks, Davidson, Holliday, Gibson, Orritt, McMordie, Irvine.

21

MILLWALL V CARLISLE UNITED

26 November 1966
The Den, London

Second Division
Attendance: 15,895

Days of destiny have come along all too rarely in Millwall's history, but this was one to savour. Over the last two seasons the Lions had gained back-to-back promotions and embarked on an outstanding run of not losing a home League match since April 1964.

Besides the goals that won the match, another essential component in Millwall's success was the input from the Lions' supporters. A few short of 16,000, they made as much noise as three times that number, and when the team needed them most, they were there. Their prompt came after Carlisle had taken a well-deserved lead, it must be said, from Eric Welsh in the 65th minute when he was singled out by the superb Willie Carlin. Cue the crowd, who now began their raucous, noisy rhythmic chant of 'Millwall! Millwall!' that reverberated around the Den enough to raise the hairs on the back of your neck. Spurred on by the atmospheric din, the Lions, who had been second best for the best part of an hour, began to

Veteran centre-forward Lennie Julians was in his swansong season as a Lion, and it was Len who scored the two goals to break Reading's long standing record, with victory over Carlisle. Len is seen here heading the winner.

stir, and for the first time in the match, Carlisle's poise and purposeful approach began to evaporate.

'I hadn't really noticed the crowd until then,' said Carlisle 'keeper Alan Ross, who was picking the ball out of the net four minutes after Carlisle had taken the lead. Millwall were back on terms when Lennie Julians connected with a corner that Ross could only partly block before seeing the ball trickle over the line.

Millwall went full throttle, stopping Carlisle in their tracks as tackles began to bite. There was no dwelling on the ball as United were pushed further and further back on defence. Despite their assurance of just 10 minutes earlier, United had now become a headless chicken, ailing and weakened by the cacophony generated by the electrifying intensity of the crowd.

Carlisle United proved stiff opposition for Millwall and their striker Dave Wilson was a real handful, as seen here challenging Millwall goalkeeper Lawrie Leslie and a watchful Tommy Wilson.

The decibels reached unbelievable levels when the frail-looking Irishman Eamon Dunphy twisted and wriggled along the byline to float over a tantalising cross for the opportunist Julians to head home the winner after 76 minutes. As 'keeper Lawrie Leslie later stated, 'You heard them, that

crowd. You couldn't let that lot down, could you? That roar gives you a lift like champagne.'

Poor old Julians was immediately engulfed by a multitude of excitable young fans, but the most defining moment of his career could have been his last as he was pinned face down on the pitch. The intervention of Harry Cripps's burly frame saved the day, wading into the pack to rescue a much-relieved Julians, and so averting a very frightening situation.

So finally, and following an absorbing encounter, Reading's 33-year-old and 55-match record had been overtaken. As for Millwall, they would extend their unbeaten home run to 59 games, before Plymouth Argyle brought the phenomenal feat to an end the following January.

Carlisle United 2   Carlisle United 1
Julians (2)   Welsh

Millwall: Leslie, Gilchrist, Cripps, Jones K., Snowdon, Wilson, Broadfoot, Hunt, Julians, Dunphy, Neil W.
Carlisle United: Ross, Neil H., Caldwell, McConnell, Passmore, Garbutt, Welsh, Carlin, Wilson, Balderstone, Hartle.

22

MILLWALL V

SHEFFIELD UNITED

13 September 1967
The Den, London

Football League Cup
Second Round
Attendance: 10,895

For many clubs like Millwall, a Cup game against a team from the First Division is an opportunity to cause an upset and a game for the fans to relish. But unlike the Middlesbrough game two seasons before, Millwall got off to the worse possible start in this game by conceding in the second minute.

The ball had been played up towards the Lions' goal when skipper Tommy Wilson yanked back the sprightly Phil Cliff as he chased the pass. As Millwall prepared their wall, United's Alan Birchenall hammered an unstoppable hit from 30 yards past a despairing Lawrie Leslie. This was how the game remained until the interval, for Millwall's attacks, despite their intensity, foundered constantly on a well-drilled and solid United defence, as the Blades seemed quite content to hold on to their lead.

Sheffield United's reluctance to kill off the game was to come back to haunt them in the second half. Millwall, despite picking up the pace and

A new one-off design for the match programme appeared in season 1967–68.

Skipper Tommy Wilson's successful penalty against the Blades was the impetus Millwall needed to go on to defeat the Yorkshire club.

getting in the Blades' faces during the first 20 minutes of the second half, never looked like scoring. That was until a foolish push by Birchenall on Millwall's Keith Weller gave them the chance to get a foot in the door.

Tommy Wilson took the captain's responsibility to smash the penalty-kick high into the net after 65 minutes. It was just the incentive that the Lions wanted, and it certainly woke the crowd up, as they began to roar the team on. From looking like sure losers, Millwall went to become likely winners, and 10 minutes later they edged in front.

Billy Neil had begun the match at inside-right, but was to prove inspirational after reverting to his normal role on the left. Powering forward at a rate of knots, Billy placed an accurate centre on to the head of the waiting Bobby Hunt, who made sure that the ball went straight in to the net. This was the signal for hundreds of youngsters to jump up and down on the pitch, much to the annoyance of everyone else. Referee Mr Spittle rebuked them with a stern warning over the tannoy, stating that if there was any reoccurrence he would abandon the game. Needless to say, it did not happen again.

United began to desperately seek an equaliser, but tempers became frayed when Wilson was booked following yet another clash with Birchenall. Five minutes remained when Millwall's other summer capture from Tottenham, Derek Posse, repaid part of his transfer fee by skilfully beating two Blades defenders to strike Millwall's third goal. There was still enough time left for the drama to continue, however. Storming forward in search of a miracle, United saw their hopes heighten briefly in the 87th minute when Bernard Shaw belted home another 30-yard effort to expose Leslie's susceptibility to long-range shots. But it all came too late for the Blades to salvage a replay.

The bottom line was that Millwall had won their first fixture of the season at home, whereas the Bramall Lane side were still waiting for an initial success on their travels.

Millwall 3   Sheffield United 2
Wilson (pen), Hunt,   Birchenall, Shaw
Possee

Millwall: Leslie, Gilchrist, Burnett, Plume (Armstrong), Kitchener, Wilson, Possee, Weller, Hunt, Dunphy, Neil.
Sheffield United: Hodgkinson, Badger, Shaw, Mallender (Woodward), Matthewson, Munks, Reece, Cliff, Jones, Birchenall, Punton.

23

BLACKBURN ROVERS V MILLWALL

7 September 1968
Ewood Park, Blackburn

Second Division
Attendance: 9,923

This victory at Ewood Park, Millwall's first at the famous Lancashire ground, coincided with Rovers losing their unbeaten home record. But any Lions fan in the crowd at Ewood Park would not have felt optimistic about Millwall's chances after watching their team concede two goals in the first 17 minutes, and it could have been more than two.

Before Rovers opened up with their salvo, Millwall's Keith Weller passed up a golden opportunity to give his team a shock lead, and Millwall fans must have feared the worse when Don Martin slammed home in the 11th minute, before lobbing Bryan King for his second six minutes later.

If an Eamon Rogers shot and a header from George Sharples had not hit the woodwork, the result, no doubt, would have gone the same way as Millwall's previous Ewood visits, all of which ended in defeats. Millwall's

Kenny Jones, with one goal and two from Harry Cripps gave the Lions their first ever win at Ewood Park.

hopes were further dashed when Billy Neil broke a finger nearing the half-hour mark and was substituted by Eamon Dunphy.

It was the Dunphy's appearance that rallied the Lions to steady the boat. This was partly achieved when they managed to reduce Rovers' lead in the 42nd minute, which came after Kenny Jones's run took him into a great position to accept Weller's inviting pass and plant his shot out of Adam Blacklaw's reach. Even this goal seemed to be just a token gesture and gave no indication that Millwall would eventually rain on Rovers' parade.

Ominously for Rovers, Millwall looked to be an entirely different proposition in the opening stages of the second half. Having managed to

wrestle midfield supremacy from Blackburn's grasp, Dunphy, Weller and Bryan Conlon began to find some leeway and space that had been originally denied them by Sharples and Barry Hole's hard and firm tackling.

Since the break, Millwall had built up a head of steam, which was to pay handsome dividends

The excellent Keith Weller registered Millwall's fourth goal at Blackburn to seal the win.

after 63 minutes when Harry Cripps turned in Conlon's knock-down for the equaliser. Rovers still had some spark left, especially up front, mainly through the persistency of both Rogers and Malcolm Darling, but the threat that they had projected early in the game began to fade.

With the game meandering to a likely draw, the Lions would have happily settled for a satisfying point, but the Rovers' defence, which had been slightly vulnerable, then collapsed like a house of cards during injury time. A Dunphy corner was only partially cleared to the waiting Cripps, who, with his back to goal, executed a glorious overhead kick that the great Pele would have been proud of. The stunned Rovers could not comprehend what had happened and seemed to be in a trance. Losing possession from the restart, they were caught slumbering again by allowing the energetic Weller to pick Sharples's pocket. The ex-Spur scampered away to casually round the advancing Blacklaw and nudge home a fourth goal, which had seemed unlikely in the first 20 minutes.

Blackburn Rovers 2   Millwall 4
Martin (2)   Jones, Cripps (2), Weller

Blackburn Rovers: Blacklaw, Newton, Wilson, Sharples, Clayton, Hole, Metcalfe, Martin, Darling, Rogers, Connelly.
Millwall: King, Gilchrist, Cripps, Jones, Kitchener, Burnett, Posse, Weller, Conlon, Jacks, Neil (Dunphy).

24

MILLWALL V BIRMINGHAM CITY

11 March 1970
The Den, London

Second Division
Attendance: 7,825

At last, to the delight of their fans, Millwall began to find some much-needed form in what had been a disappointing season that had yielded just six League wins up to the turn of the year. But after defeating the champions elect, Huddersfield Town, Millwall would go on to exceed their total of victories by winning seven of their 10 remaining fixtures, including this thrashing of Birmingham City.

The Den was again a sodden morass and it was a wonder that the game ever started, as both penalty areas lay under pools of water. Once play commenced, however, the deluge soon evaporated under the feet of 22 players. The soggy conditions did not prevent a rampant Millwall, ably lead by the marvellous Keith Weller, from attacking from the first whistle. The Lions excelled with their excellent use of long ball – ideal given the state of the pitch. Millwall's accurate passing was quite uncanny, whereas City got bogged down with their pedestrian build-up of short passes. But it was City who should have taken the lead in the 10th minute. Their first promising move ended eight yards from Millwall's goal when Geoff Vowden could only place his header straight at goalkeeper Bryan King. Moments later, King was brought into action once more to deny Bert Murray's 25-yard thunderbolt with a superb save.

Millwall found their range when Derek Possee clouted a post after 18 minutes, before they took the lead two minutes later. City defender Dave Robinson's inadequate back pass was held up in the mire, and he could only watch in despair as Gordon Bolland scooted past him to beat the advancing Dave Latchford. It was 2–0 after 29 minutes when 18-year-old Doug Allder's exceptional and brave run took him through two tackles to give Possee the chance to score through the crowded goalmouth.

The Lions were cruising, but inadvertently handed Birmingham a lifeline, with City scoring twice in three minutes. A harmless-looking cross from Murray was unnecessarily handled by Dennis Burnett, leaving Murray to finish off his initial handiwork by converting the penalty-kick. Incredibly, Millwall conceded another soft goal that brought City level in the 40th minute. A Malcolm Beard centre took a fortunate ricochet off an unknowing teammate and found a waiting Trevor Hockey to gleefully tap home.

From the moment that Millwall scored, two minutes into the second half, there would be no more parity in this particular game. With the fans hardly settled in their seats, Bolland landed his second goal, a classy header from Weller's cross. The remainder of the game would be solely a Millwall preserve, and they went 4–2 up in the 58th minute. It was the forceful Bolland who sealed his first Millwall hat-trick after Weller's shot had been partially cleared.

Millwall's free-flowing football made light of the muddy pitch, and the magical Bolland nearly scored a fourth goal, but his header was cleared off the line. His next piece of individuality came with 16 minutes left; Bolland found his co-tormentor, Weller, with an excellent pass, for Weller to run on and thump home the fifth goal past Latchford. City's overworked defence had found it difficult to pin Bolland down, they then had Dave Latchford to thank again for keeping another of the effervescent Bolland's free-kicks from hitting the back of the net.

In the 84th minute the rout was completed with a rare but deserved goal from Eamon Dunphy's header following a Weller cross for goal number six. Millwall's performance, especially in the second half, had mesmerised Birmingham, and it must have left them wondering what had hit them. This was the first time that Millwall had scored six goals at the Den since defeating Notts County 6–1 nearly six years before, and it was a pity that the smallest attendance of the season was there to witness such a fabulous Millwall display of fluent, enterprising and exuberant football.

Millwall 6   Birmingham City 2
Bolland (3), Possee,   Murray (pen), Hockey
Weller, Dunphy

Millwall: King, Brown B., Cripps, Dorney, Kitchener, Burnett, Possee, Dunphy, Bolland, Weller, Allder.
Birmingham City: Latchford, Martin, Thomson, Pendry, Robinson, Beard, Murray, Vincent, Vowden, Hockey, Summerill.

25

QUEEN'S PARK RANGERS V MILLWALL

18 November 1972
Loftus Road, London

Second Division
Attendance: 15,837

When Millwall lost at Nottingham Forest at the beginning of November, they descended to the foot of the table amid many recriminations, one of which was the lack of investment in the team during the close season. The club's critics seemed to have valid reasons for their gripes; however, the Lions had created enough chances at the City Ground to at least garner a point, before eventually going down by the odd goal in five.

The inclusion of the Irish international Eamon Dunphy assisted greatly in turning a negative into a positive, and saw Millwall enter an unbeaten run of seven matches until Fulham defeated them on Boxing Day. Included in this sequence was the splendid victory over Queen's Park Rangers in West London. The manager of the Hoops was Gordon Jago, who a little over two years later would find himself in the hot seat at Cold Blow Lane.

Rangers' push for promotion had gone off the rails of late; their defensive frailties had been shown up after shipping in nine goals in the last five games – this in stark contrast to the previous five fixtures, where they had not conceded any.

So, with Rangers in an autumnal crisis, Millwall felt that their opponents were ripe for the picking. The very first goal of what was to be a rich harvest came after a mere 31 seconds. Straight from the kick-off the ball found its way to Steve Brown, free on the right. With plenty of space to attack, the young Lions winger left Ian Evans floundering, and when Hoops defender Tony Hazell failed to clear Brown's powerful cross, it found Gordon Bolland, who promptly fired home the opening goal from just inside the area.

The encouraging start was more than Millwall could have hoped for, and things were to get a whole lot better on the half-hour mark when the Lions went two up. On this occasion, the attack commenced down the left flank after a Rangers move had broken down. Outside-left Dougie Allder got possession to take on and brush aside Hazell's woeful challenge to beat Phil Parkes from 20 yards with a fierce drive.

Momentarily Millwall's resolve was put to the test when Rangers pulled a goal back three minutes later. Dave Thomas placed his corner to the near post, where the enigmatic Stan Bowles was waiting to head past Bryan King. But Millwall were in no mood to let a deserved lead slip any further. The two-goal margin was restored with a stylish strike in the 36th minute. The goal was a shot of stunning velocity that came from an unlikely source – the marvellous and inspirational captain, Dennis Burnett. Receiving the ball some 30 yards from goal, Burnett set himself to launch a rocket that whizzed past a startled Parkes for Millwall's third goal.

Going into the interval on the back of an excellent 45 minutes of football, the Lions had showed that superior teamwork would prevail over a side reliant on the attributes of individual players. The second half, however, would show whether Millwall had truly turned the corner, or if Rangers could up their game with a change of tactics and produce a much better showing.

Millwall's defence was breached just once on their trip to West London and here Stan Bowles beats Harry Cripps to head past Bryan King. However, it did not stop the Lions obtaining a splendid victory over Rangers.

Early in the second period, the home side had the chance to redeem themselves in the 52nd minute when the impish and hard-working Bowles shuttled into the Millwall area, but his run was curtailed when Bryan King, the Lions 'keeper, raced from his line to clear the danger, but his momentum carried him into the wily Mancunian to concede a penalty. The allotted task was handed to Don Givens, and although the Irishman's accuracy was spot on, the power was deficiently amiss, leaving King to execute a fine save at the expense of a corner.

It was no more than Millwall deserved, but it left Rangers fairly dispirited. As manager Jago reported, 'If there was going to be a turning point in the game, it was in the second half when we missed a penalty'. But credit must go to the West Londoners; although not playing particularly well, they gave it a go, especially when the Lions sat on their lead. Rangers' tenacity towards the end of the game was mainly thanks to the efforts of Rangers striker Mick Leach, who became the main threat to Millwall's lead for the remainder of the match. Belated offerings from Thomas and Leach were a slight concern to King, but generally the Millwall 'keeper was equal to anything that the Rangers' attack could conjure up. In spite of Rangers attacking for most of the second half, it was their failure to create and capitalise on the accruing opportunities was the main reason for their defeat.

Rangers would have to return to the drawing board; nonetheless, the defeat to Millwall would not upset Rangers' chances in the least, as they gained promotion by claiming the runner-up spot. But the discrepancy between the top and the bottom of the League table had been exposed by Millwall's excellent display, which ended Rangers' unbeaten home run.

The win was also the fillip that the Lions needed to make a steady progress up the table, and it saw them finish in 11th place. This they achieved with the contribution of a remarkably small squad, of which 12 players only would make 25 or more appearances over the course of the season.

Queen's Park Rangers 1   Millwall 3
Bowles   Bolland, Allder, Burnett

Queen's Park Rangers: Parkes, Clement, Gillard, Venables, Evans (O'Rourke), Hazell, Thomas, Francis, Leach, Bowles, Givens.
Millwall: King, Brown B., Cripps, Dorney, Kitchener, Burnett, Brown S., Bolland, Wood, Dunphy, Allder.

26

MILLWALL V

SOUTHAMPTON

12 October 1974   **Second Division**
The Den, London   **Attendance: 9,306**

Heading into this match, Millwall had acquired a pitiful three wins out of 12 games, and this stuttering start had already thrown up the first casualties in what would become a desperate season. Following chairman Mickey Purser's departure, it was inevitable that manager Benny Fenton would go too, now that his benefactor had left.

Left holding the baby and put in charge of first-team affairs was coach and the former player, Lawrie Leslie. His first game at the helm would be against Southampton, and in his pre-match edict Leslie had promised that the Lions would go for an all-out attack from the start. The caretaker manager was true to his word, as Millwall proceeded to give a heart-warming and encouraging performance, and one that would see Leslie throw his hat into the ring for the manager's job.

Nonetheless, Southampton had come into the game on the back of a splendid midweek 5–0 League Cup thrashing of First Division Derby County and, with just 9 goals scored so far, Millwall's immediate

Above: Southampton's Bob McCarthy took man-to-man marking to an excess when tussling with Millwall's Doug Allder.

Millwall's Alf Wood seems very amused by sitting on Saints goalkeeper who appears to be unimpressed.

prospects looked far from promising. In the opening phase, the Saints seemed like they were going to carry on from where they left off against the Rams, but two early misses by Hugh Fisher were to set the pattern for the rest of Southampton's afternoon.

The Den was bathed in mid-autumnal sunshine, and the sun was certainly shining on Millwall in the 14th minute. It was full-back cum midfielder Dave Donaldson who was instrumental in supplying the through ball for Brian Clark to curl home a sweet left-foot effort. The match got even better five minutes later, when Doug Allder's run into the area was brought to a juddering halt by Saints goalkeeper Ian Turner's rugby tackle. Turner's reward was to fish the ball out of the net after Gordon Bolland sent him the wrong way from the penalty spot.

Ian Turner in the Southampton goal had no answer to prevent Gordon Bolland from scoring a second penalty in his team's 4–0 defeat.

Brian Clark also scored a brace against the Saints and is seen here lashing home his first past Ian Turner.

Despite their deficiencies at the back, the Saints, with Peter Osgood, Mike Channon and Bobby Stokes, still had enough in their locker to worry the Lions, and Stokes confirmed their attacking presence with a dipping volley that forced Bryan King into an excellent tip-over.

After the early scares had passed, and with two goals in the bank, Millwall settled into a pleasing rhythm and began to pulverise the Southampton defence. They came close to stretching their lead when former Saint Frank Saul saw his effort hacked off the line by Paul Bennett, with Millwall seemingly capable of scoring every time they threatened the Southampton goal.

The second half saw Millwall continue to dominate in much the same vein as the first. A further bout of prolonged pressure was handsomely rewarded on 60 minutes when the Southampton defence conceded a third goal. It came following another clinical move that ended when Millwall's Alf Wood's effort was blocked, only for the ball to fall invitingly for strike partner Brian Clark to hammer home his second goal of the game. Five minutes later, the match ceased to be a contest when the Lions were awarded a second spot-kick.

Big centre-half Barry Kitchener, who had remained in the Southampton area following a corner, seemed surprised to receive the ball, and before he could use it, he had his legs taken away by Bob McCarthy's clumsy challenge. That left Gordon Bolland the formality of stroking home another immaculate penalty for goal number four and giving Millwall their biggest victory of the season so far. Caretaker manager Lawrie Leslie stating, 'I am over the moon. Everything I had planned worked, with the players being in the right positions at the right time.'

Unfortunately, this success did not kick-start Millwall's ascent up the table, as they had to wait another two months before eking out another win. Even the appointment of Gordon Jago as the new manager in late October failed to inspire the team, and as a consequence Millwall were eventually relegated.

Millwall 4   Southampton 0
Clark (2)
Bolland (2 pens)

Millwall: King, Brown B., Jones E., Donaldson, Kitchener, Dorney, Saul, Bolland, Wood, Clark, Allder.
Southampton: Turner, McCarthy, Peach, Fisher, Bennett, Mills (Blyth), Stokes, Channon, Osgood, Holmes, Steele.

27

MILLWALL V BRIGHTON & HOVE ALBION

16 April 1976
The Den, London

Third Division
Attendance: 23,008

Had you asked any Millwall supporter at the start of the season the question 'what are the odds of the Lions going up?', quite a few would have replied pessimistically, especially after the departure of goalkeeper Bryan King to Coventry City and Manchester United's capture of the mercurial left-winger Gordon Hill.

So when Millwall entertained Brighton on Good Friday 1976, the club found themselves in with a decent shout at promotion, it was much to the surprise and delight of their fans.

This important victory over fellow contenders Brighton & Hove Albion put them into one of the three automatic promotion places. Cold Blow Lane's biggest crowd for four years saw a very tense encounter in which the stalemate went unbroken until the 43rd minute.

The outcome of the match could have gone in a completely different direction in the first half, had Millwall goalkeeper Ray Goddard not been on his mettle. Brighton, lacking four first-team regulars, including former

Trevor Lee's acrobatics gave Millwall the lead against Brighton in the Good Friday encounter at The Den.

Lion Dennis Burnett, looked the more composed team at first. It was Goddard's athletic leap from Albion's Brian Horton's vicious dipping volley that kept the score at 0–0.

The opening goal was one of classic finishing: a Dave Donaldson cross was helped on by John Seasman for Trevor Lee to power his excellent bicycle kick past Albion goalkeeper Peter Grummitt. The second goal was scored right on the interval, when a Phil Summerill cross was met by Albion right-back Joe Kinnear, whose attempted header lacked the necessary purchase and gave Seasman the chance to nip in for goal number two. It was only the fourth time in the season that the Lions had scored two goals in the first half.

Millwall's find of the season was Lee's former Epsom teammate, Phil Walker, who is seen challenging Albion's Fred Binney for the ball.

Brighton were undone for a third time on the hour, when Terry Brisley cracked home a half-volley from the edge of the area after Steve Piper had headed out Phil Walker's centre. This gave Millwall a comfortable three-goal cushion, until Albion pulled one back when substitute Gerry Fell laid it on a plate for Fred Binney to net from close range in the 86th minute.

Following his earlier heroics, the Lions 'keeper caught a dose of the jitters late in the game – his fumbling resembled a drunk attempting to catch a balloon. It was just as well for Goddard that the rest of the defence did not follow suit, although Brighton's attack were not nearly sharp enough to take advantage.

The Lions maintained their superb run by winning their last two fixtures, but then had to endure an agonising wait to see if their total of 56 points would be enough. Eventually it was, as Millwall went up, and not their neighbours and rivals Crystal Palace, despite Palace looking like a certainty at Christmas.

One anomaly to surface at the end of the season was that Phil Summerill, with eight League goals, finished joint leading goalscorer along with Gordon Hill, whose last Millwall strike came against Colchester United on 1 November. This fact alone would seem to justify the fans' less than optimistic view of why Millwall would not feature in any promotion race.

The Lions' goal tally of just 56 goals scored was the second lowest of the top dozen teams in the Division, even relegated Southend mustered 65. But defensively they were strong and conceded a mere 43 goals, the lowest of all 24 clubs. This figure illustrates the quality and resolve of the team when it really mattered.

Millwall 3   Brighton & Hove Albion 1
Lee, Seasman, Brisley   Binney

Millwall: Goddard, Donaldson, Moore, Brisley, Kitchener, Hazell, McGrath, Seasman, Summerill, Walker, Lee.
Brighton & Hove Albion: Grummitt, Kinnear, Wilson, Horton, Rollings, Piper, Towner, O'Sullivan, Binney, Ward, Mellor (Fell).

28

MILLWALL V WOLVERHAMPTON WANDERERS

1 January 1977   **Second Division**
The Den, London   **Attendance: 16,928**

This exceptional game was the perfect remedy for those suffering a New Year hangover, as two excellent teams fought tooth and nail at a rain-soaked Cold Blow Lane, where Millwall gave their best performance since beating Chelsea 3–0 earlier in the season and were unfortunate not to claim both points.

A full-blooded first half saw Millwall take the game to Wolves, and nearly scored when Jon Moore finished off a fine five-pass move with a piledriver that skimmed the Wanderers' crossbar. Trevor Lee then showed his heading prowess twice in as many minutes when his back header was diverted clear by Geoff Palmer, before Chris Parkin foiled Lee's other goal-bound effort.

After weathering Millwall's onslaught, promotion favourites Wolves showed exactly how they had scored 51 goals in 21 games. There was a

decent slice of good fortune that brought them the opening goal in the 44th minute; the goal came when Lions defender Tony Hazell appeared to have Steve Daley's pass covered, but the ball hit a divot to fall nicely for John Richards to tee up Kenny Hibbitt, who made no mistake in netting the goal.

Mounting pressure from Millwall brought some panic to the Wolves rearguard that saw Kenny Hibbert nearly decapitate his own goalkeeper Gary Pierce.

Building on their success, Wanderers began to pound Millwall early in the second half and were nearly rewarded with a second goal when Steve Kindon cracked his 54th-minute shot against the Millwall crossbar. Two minutes later, Kindon probably realised that it was not going to be his day when Hazell again erred. This time, the Lions defender's headed clearance went straight to Kindon, and from point-blank range Lions 'keeper Ray Goddard brought off a miraculous save.

Midfielders Pat Sharkey of Millwall and Kenny Hibbert [Wolves] become a little excited as the battle for supremacy intensified.

As the midfield struggle intensified, tempers became heated as Pat Sharkey and Hibbitt squared up to each other, as did Terry Brisley and Steve Daley, whose remonstration with the referee earned him a booking. Millwall then brought on substitute Phil Walker for the injured Barrie Fairbrother in the 62nd minute. Walker's impact was immediate and saw Millwall regain some of their earlier impetus, and with 17 minutes to go they finally and deservedly drew level.

Whatever central-defender Tony Hazell was doing taking a corner, Millwall's 12th, no one will ever know, but over it came and there was Trevor Lee rising above the throng to firmly head home past a gallant Gary Pierce. Just as the goal went in, a cloudburst descended on the Den, which turned an already saturated pitch into a morass.

The conditions were treacherous and no one would have blamed Millwall for being a tad more cautious, but, with little time remaining, both teams went willingly forward to seek a winner. It was all to no avail, however, as the final whistle was blown and the pitch alone was left to the mercy of the worsening precipitation.

Trevor Lee gave Millwall a deserved equaliser in the draw with Wolves on a very wet New Year's Day clash at The Den.

So ended a classic contest that had been played in unremitting rain throughout. Those fortunate to be there witnessed entertainment of the highest quality from both teams, who adapted magnificently in difficult circumstances. In manager Jago's words, 'It was a superb match and a draw was probably a fair result. I couldn't have asked for more from my team.'

Millwall 1   Wolverhampton Wanderers 1
Lee   Hibbitt

Millwall: Goddard, Evans, Donaldson, Brisley, Kitchener, Hazell, Lee, Seasman, Sharkey, Moore, Fairbrother (Walker).
Wolverhampton Wanderers: Pierce, Palmer, Parkin, Daley, Munro, McAlle, Hibbitt, Richards, Sunderland, Kindon, Patching.

29

MILLWALL V MANSFIELD TOWN

2 May 1978
The Den, London

Second Division
Attendance: 9,187

The trials and tribulations that Millwall encountered in the aftermath of the violence at the Ipswich Town FA Cup tie, and the Football Association's decision to levy a 14-day closure of the Den could have had severe repercussions as the Lions fought a desperate battle against relegation.

Brighton had been the selected venue for the Mansfield game, but Albion withdrew their permission after coming under pressure from the local South Coast residents group and Hove Corporation. The Millwall club, through no fault of their own, had now been branded outcasts, with other clubs unwilling to solve another's problems.

Although Portsmouth's Fratton Park had held the home fixture versus Bristol Rovers on the Saturday, which had passed off relatively trouble-free, the idea of having any Millwall supporters, let alone the yobs, parading around the Sussex town the following Wednesday night filled the locals and their authority with trepidation. Brighton's volte-face had come at very short notice, and it left the Football League with no other option but to

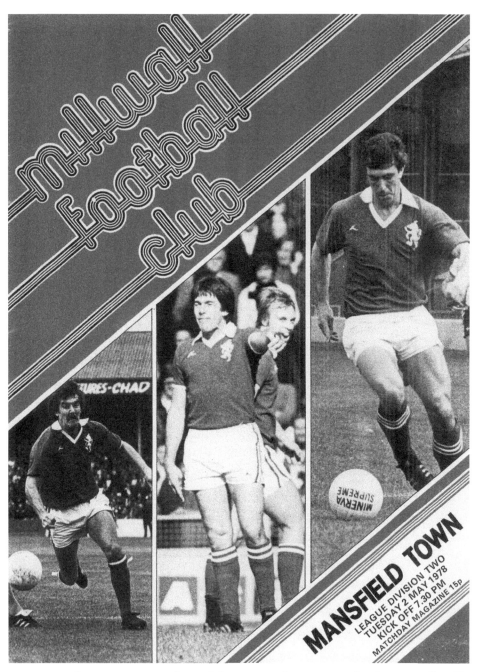

postpone the game. As other clubs seemed unsympathetic to Millwall's predicament, any new date set for the game would surely fall after the 14-day ban had expired. Not counting their chickens too soon, it was the best news that the trouble-torn Lions had received recently. A few days later, the

Rod Arnold's penalty save from Tony Hazell in 16th minute only added to the tension in a must win game for the Lions.

authorities confirmed that the outstanding game would indeed take place at the Den.

The players had responded magnificently to the club's plight, and following the defeat at Stoke City, remained solely focused on the job in hand. There was just six games left – five of them at home, including Mansfield – and in order to survive they had to win them all. When the Stags finally arrived at the Den, a month after they were originally destined for the Sussex Coast, the Lions, against all expectations, had won the previous five games. All they needed now was victory in this final encounter to secure their Second Division status.

The game was never going to be a classic, the conditions made sure of that, with pools of water laying on the pitch on a damp, soggy New Cross evening. Rain had been falling all day, and early doubts of the match taking place were proved groundless when referee Tom Reynolds stated that there was no question of a postponement.

John Seasman's headed goal broke the deadlock and proved to be the winner in a very tense match with Mansfield Town, which enable Millwall to survive the drop.

Tension was rife among the crowd, but Millwall quickly got into their stride. Following some early pressure, the Lions were awarded a penalty-kick after 16 minutes thanks to Kevin Bird's tug on John Seasman's shirt. Step forward Tony Hazell, Millwall's penalty hero against Oldham at the weekend, but the groans that greeted Rod Arnold's save could have been heard down the Old Kent Road.

The miss did no one's blood pressure any good, and neither did Ian Pearson's failure to score six minutes later. He fastened on to a long punt from Barry Kitchener and, after rounding Stags 'keeper Arnold, lost his footing with the gaping chasm of a goal in front of him. Colin Foster then sent the stress levels into the stratosphere when his snap shot was saved at full stretch by Lions 'keeper Nicky Johns. Then, in the 40th minute, all the pent-up frustrations were relieved when Seasman rose to meet Bryan Hamilton's free-kick to powerfully head home one of the most crucial goals in the club's history.

Millwall seemed content with their slender lead, and around the hour mark manager George Petchey brought on teenage prodigy Dave Mehmet for the flagging Pearson, which did not sit very well with the fans. With the nerves already frayed and fingernails bitten to the quick, Mansfield brought further agitation when Gordon Hodgson was a whisker away from converting Bird's centre as the Stags began to press. Looking like the stronger side, Mansfield began to threaten the Millwall goal with their best spell of the game. But, having weathered Mansfield's menace, the Lions produced a late flurry in which they nearly scored again. Four minutes remained when Seasman broke free along the byline, looking up to find the waiting Trevor Lee. But his effort was pushed out of harms way by Arnold, leaving the fans to fret for just a few moments longer.

So, finally, a campaign that began high in confidence but came close to derailment by the debauchery of hooliganism was resurrected by exceptional resilience, and relegation was unexpectedly staved off.

Millwall 1   Mansfield Town 0
Seasman

Millwall: Johns, Donaldson, Moore, Allen, Kitchener, Hazell, Lee, Hamilton, Seasman, Walker, Pearson (Mehmet).
Mansfield Town: Arnold, Pate, Foster B., Foster C., Saxby, Bird, Millar, Martin, Syrett, Hodgson, Goodwin.

30

MILLWALL V

SHREWSBURY TOWN

5 January 1980   **FA Cup Third Round**
The Den, London   **Attendance: 7,026**

After their less than impressive and wholly unconvincing display against Croydon in round two, the fans could be forgiven for asking what Millwall team would turn up for this clash with Second Division Shrewsbury Town. Well, following a sparkling 90-minute football extravaganza, the answer was: an exceptional one.

Millwall made very hard work of beating Croydon, but against Shrewsbury they were totally unrecognisable. Looking hungry, and with a renewed appetite, they shone brightly and performed with a great deal of vigour.

Most of the exuberance on show came from the selection of five members from the previous season's FA Youth Cup-winning 11. One of those talented youngsters was outside-left Kevin O'Callaghan; he and his partner on the right flank, Tony Towner, became the main conduits for the Lions to rack up their five goals.

An early goal is a great boost, especially in a Cup tie, and Millwall got theirs after 15 minutes when a Phil Coleman drive was cleared as far as

Above: Welsh striker Johnny Lyons was well on the way to becoming a Lions legend, helped in no small way with three cracking goals in the romp over Shrewsbury Town. Here is his first.

Right: John's fine angled drive secured his second against the Salop.

Bottom right: then a superbly struck volley brought John his hat-trick, with all the goals coming at the Cold Blow Lane end of The Den.

O'Callaghan, whose punt at goal appeared to be going wide until the ever-alert Alan McKenna diverted it past Shrewsbury 'keeper Bob Wardle. This was McKenna's first senior goal for the club after returning from a career-threatening cartilage operation.

The Lions had virtually put their name in the hat for the next round when centre-back Tony Tagg headed home a Dave Mehmet free-kick in the 28th minute. Shrewsbury hit back by forcing eight corners in a 10-minute spell, which came to a halt when Towner set off a mesmerising 50-yard run that left five defenders floundering, before forcing Wardle to make a fine save.

If the first half had been worth the entrance money then the second 45 minutes would have cost the equivalent of a season ticket. The Lions fans were up and cheering again in the 58th minute when Colin Griffin upended McKenna. The free-kick was left for Johnny Lyons to thunder home a shot of stunning quality and venom, finding the top corner of Wardle's net.

Five minutes had elapsed when Lyons, at his predatory best, fired home Towner's low cross at the second attempt for Millwall's fourth. Shrewsbury were denied moments later when Mel Blyth cleared one of the visitors' rare efforts off the line.

By now Millwall were calling all the shots, with one assault closely followed by another, so it came as no surprise when they scored again. John Lyons claimed his first and only hat-trick for the Lions with a lethal volley from six yards. Chances were coming thick and fast as Millwall went seeking their biggest win of the season, but it was curtailed when Paul Maguire claimed some consolation for Shrewsbury with another stunning goal and brought down the curtain on an exceptional FA Cup tie, with Shrewsbury player-manager Graham Turner saying, 'Millwall gave us a lesson in how to finish and how to defend. Even when the score was 5–0 they were defending as though their lives depended on it.'

Millwall's dramatic victory was unfortunately marred when a missile hit and knocked out one of the linesmen, Mr Leonard Hopper, who lay prone for several minutes before he was revived. This was the last thing the club needed, especially as the last punishment order meted out by the Football Association following the crowd trouble against Ipswich Town in 1978 had just expired.

In keeping with such a topsy-turvy campaign, Millwall went tamely out of the competition to Chester in round four.

Millwall 5   Shrewsbury Town 1
McKenna, Tagg,   Maguire
Lyons (3)

Millwall: Jackson, Coleman (Kitchener), Roberts, Mehmet, Tagg, Blyth, Towner, Seasman, McKenna, Lyons, O'Callaghan.
Shrewsbury Town: Wardle, King, Larkin, Turner, Griffin (Cross), Keay, Tong, Atkins, Biggins, Dungworth, Maguire.

31

MILLWALL V

SWINDON TOWN

4 March 1980
The Den, London

Third Division
Attendance: 6,572

Millwall gave their most scintillating performance of the season, in which Lions outside-right Tony 'Tiger' Towner emphasised what a gifted and talented player he was and the important part he would play if Millwall were to make a late charge for promotion. He gave former Southampton left-back David Peach, who was making his debut for the Robins following his £150,000 move, such a torrid evening that the ex-Saint may have wished that he had stayed at the Dell. Time after time, the fleet-footed Tiger skipped past him with ease to hit a string of telling crosses that strikers Johnny Lyons and Bobby Shinton would relish.

The goal glut got underway in the 10th minute, when Towner sped past Peach to deliver a perfect centre for centre-back Tony Tagg to head home at the back post. The Robins were then given the opportunity to level when Mel Blyth was penalised for handball. Up stepped Ray McHale to hit hard and low, but he was foiled by goalkeeper John Jackson's superb save down to his left after 23 minutes.

Johnny Lyons sends his free-kick over Swindon's defensive wall and past goalkeeper Jimmy Allen to register Millwall's fifth goal in the rout of the Robins.

Millwall went two up after 31 minutes when Shinton collected a loose ball just outside the penalty area to beat advancing Swindon goalie Jimmy Allan with an exquisite chip. A minute later, Swindon hauled themselves back into contention when Alan Mayes' fine run and cross was met by Andy Rowland, who prodded home his 22nd goal of the season from close range.

The Robins had hardly had time to celebrate when Millwall regained their two-goal cushion in the 38th minute. An audacious flick from Lyons sent Towner scampering through the middle of Swindon's rapidly disappearing rearguard to finish clinically under Allan's late dive. Two minutes later, Lyons was again involved when setting up his former Wrexham colleague, Shinton, who headed home the Welshman's deep cross for the fourth, which brought the half to an end.

The action continued into the second half, with the Lions well in command, and they strengthened their grip on the game to go further ahead in the 61st minute. Millwall midfielder Tony Kinsella was flattened by Swindon's Chris Kamara on the edge of the area, but retribution was swift when dead-ball specialist Johnny Lyons sent a marvellous curling

Swindon Town felt the force of Millwall attacking instincts with North Walian John Lyons [far right] helping himself to a brace and is seen here completing the scoring with the Lions sixth goal.

free-kick over the Robins' defensive wall and into the net for goal number five. The visitors drew some consolation from the wreckage when Mayes' speculative long-range shot was deflected in off Lions full-back John Sitton.

But it was Millwall who had the final say in the 87th minute, when a short corner routine between Paul Roberts and

Another two-goal hero was Bobby Shinton who's pace unnerved the Robins defence all night. This photo, however, shows another Shinton effort go wide.

Kinsella found Manchester City loanee Shinton free in the area to power a low drive into the path of Lyons, to touch home from close range.

Millwall were a class act in this match, manager Petchey quoted as saying, 'Who could write off our promotion chances after that performance? Some of our football was absolutely brilliant.' It was a good game, but it would sum up their season in a nutshell; inconsistent to the last, they would win only another two games (both at home) out of the 14 remaining to finish a disappointing 14th place.

Millwall 6   Swindon Town 2
Tagg, Shinton (2)   Rowland, Sitton (og)
Towner, Lyons (2)

Millwall: Jackson, Sitton, Roberts, Chatterton, Tagg, Blyth (Coleman), Towner, Seasman, Shinton, Lyons, Kinsella.
Swindon Town: Allan, Lewis, Peach, McHale, Tucker (Carter), Stroud, Bates, Kamara, Rowland, Mayes, Williams.

32

EXETER CITY V MILLWALL

3 October 1981
St James Park, Exeter

Third Division
Attendance: 7,169

Millwall appeared dead and buried at 5–1 down with just 20 minutes to play in this game, but fought back with so much tenacity that they nearly made it back to New Cross with what would have been an astonishing draw from an epic thriller of a game.

It took Exeter just three minutes to open their account when John Delve's free-kick to the near post found Tony Kellow, who bravely headed home his fifth goal of the season. The Lions went two down from another set piece in the 20th minute, in which Delve was heavily involved. After being fouled by Sam Allardyce, Delve received Frank Prince's free-kick to float over a cross to Peter Rogers, who nodded back for Mike Lester to force the ball home from six yards.

It got worse two minutes later when Delve, relishing the space in midfield, picked up Kellow's fine pass to fire in a shot that skimmed off Lester, past startled Millwall goalkeeper Peter Gleasure. The Lions rallied to claw back a goal in the 32nd minute when Allardyce nodded on a Tony Tagg free-kick for Dean Horrix to score with an exquisite flick that dropped over the head of City 'keeper Len Bond.

Exeter hat-trick hero Mike Lester gets between Tony Tagg and Chris Dibble to open his account in the nine goal thriller.

The Lions thought that they had scored a second goal five minutes before the break when Nick Chatterton's header hit the underside of the bar and appeared to go over the line, but referee Kieran Barrett waved play on, much to the visitors' annoyance. Exeter increased their lead seven minutes after the restart when Lester completed his hat-trick with a simple tap-in after Joe Cooke had done all the groundwork.

When City's ex-Portsmouth winger Dave Pullar set up Rogers to score the fifth goal in the 68th minute, it appeared that Millwall were going to be on the wrong end of a massive hiding. But within four minutes the Lions began their incredible fightback when player-manager Peter Anderson thumped home a centre from Horrix. Ten minutes later, they scored a third when Bond failed to cut Chatterton's corner-kick to allow Tagg to head home.

Throwing caution to the wind, Millwall, with all guns blazing, created a frenzied last eight minutes and were awarded a penalty in injury time when Martyn Rogers was pulled up for handball. Nicky Chatterton slammed home the resultant spot-kick. Had this goal come minutes earlier, who knows what the final outcome would have been...

Exeter City 5	Millwall 4
Kellow, Lester (3),	Horrix, Anderson, Tagg,
Rogers P.	Chatterton (pen)

Exeter City: Bond, Rogers M., Sparrow, Lester, Cooke, Roberts L., Rogers P., Prince, Kellow, Delve, Pullar.
Millwall: Gleasure, Roberts P., Warman, Chatterton, Tagg, Martin, Dibble, Anderson, Horrix, Bartley, West (Massey)

33

CHESTERFIELD V MILLWALL

14 May 1983
Recreation Ground,
Chesterfield

Third Division
Attendance: 4,314

Since their relegation in 1979, Millwall had been drifting aimlessly around the Third Division like a rudderless ship, seemingly heading for the rocks. The incumbent manager at the time was George Petchey, who in nearly three years had failed to revitalise the club. Petchey was replaced by Peter Anderson in December 1980, who took on the dual role of player-manager.

Anderson had trained as a chartered accountant, but was also a very skillful midfield performer. At the time it appeared to be a very good appointment, with someone who could play a bit and balance the books at the same time. A ninth-place finish in his first full season (1981–82), however, was seen as a marked improvement. The prospects looked a lot better for the 1982–83 season, especially when a recognised striker, the Bermondsey-born Trevor Aylott, was recruited from Barnsley.

Unfortunately, following a poor run of results the writing was on the wall for Pete. It saw him and his assistant, Terry Long, relieved of their duties prior to the match at Wigan in November 1982. Early in December the new manager was revealed – it was to be George Graham, the Queen's Park Rangers coach, who was taking his first step on the managerial ladder.

With Millwall in freefall, Graham could not have taken on board a more onerous task than he had at Cold Blow Lane. It was a month before he registered his initial victory and, with just three wins in 16 matches, the position was just as precarious as when he took over. The team was in need of some urgent remedial work. Discarding the underachievers, Graham began his surgery by bringing in over half a dozen players in a matter of weeks, who had not only the ruggedness, but also the mental toughness required to dig the club out of one almighty hole.

After a brief bedding-in process, Graham's influence began to flourish, with a surge of seven victories in an excellent run of just one defeat in 11 games. Despite their new-found form, survival would hinge on securing a win in the final game at Chesterfield if they did not want to accompany the already relegated Spireites into the Fourth Division for the first time in 18 years.

From the outset, in an incident-packed game Millwall displayed no nervous anxiety

Skipper Dave Cusack who scored the penalty against an already relegated Chesterfield is seen here challenging Martin Henderson for possession.

as they pinned the home team back on defence, forcing four corners in the first dozen minutes as the Lions sought an early breakthrough. Chesterfield's initial response did not arrive until the 25th minute, when Andy Higginbottom played in Mick Gooding, but his effort was nullified by Lions goalkeeper Peter Wells getting his angles right.

Despite their first-half superiority, Millwall had to wait until the 33rd minute before a sniff of a goal presented itself, when Paul Robinson's dipping drive from the edge of the penalty area struck the crossbar. The Spireites hit back with efforts from Gooding, which Wells did well to smother at the striker's feet, before Calvin Plummer shot wide from close range.

As the half drew to a close, a colour clash of sorts occurred in the 43rd minute when Millwall's Dean White appeared to headbutt the Chesterfield skipper, Bill Green, who retaliated in kind, and both were promptly despatched for an early bath by referee Jeff Bray. A downpour during the interval failed to stop Millwall from pressing ahead early in the second half, and, with three-quarters of the game played, the all-important goal arrived in the 66th minute.

The goal arose when Otulakowksi began one of his familiar mazy runs, which took him into the Chesterfield area, induced a reckless tackle and brought the inevitable award of a penalty-kick. Taking his captain's role to the extreme, Dave Cusack sent his kick high and wide of Mike Turner's dive and into the net.

Chesterfield's forays thereafter were ineffective, mainly due to Plummer being continuously caught offside by Millwall's well-drilled defence. Two minutes from time, the game was held up when a few hundred of the travelling supporters went on to the pitch thinking that the game was over, when the official had only blown for a free-kick. It took the police several minutes to clear the pitch before the game resumed and came to a satisfactory conclusion.

Incredibly, this victory was only Millwall's second success on the road; the first had not come until their 37th fixture of the season; 3–2 at the Orient on Easter Monday. This reprieve saw Millwall advance rather quickly under Graham, and saw them consolidate to take ninth place in the 1983–84 season, before finishing runners-up to Bradford City and gaining promotion to Division Two in 1985.

Chesterfield 0   Millwall 1
                        Cusack (pen)

Chesterfield: Turner, Stirk, Pollard, Kowalski, Green, Bellamy, Plummer, Partridge, Gooding, Henderson (Brown), Higginbottom.
Millwall: Wells, Lovell, Stride, White, Nutton, Cusack, Bremner, Massey (McLeary), Robinson, Otulakowski, Madden.

34

READING V

MILLWALL

13 February 1988
Elm Park, Reading

Second Division
Attendance: 6,050

Having lost their last two League games against the City teams of Birmingham and Bradford, Millwall were on course to lose a third when trailing 2–1 at the break at Reading.

For relegation-haunted Reading, it all began so well in the first half. They had striker Billy Whitehurst making his debut after joining from Oxford United. The big Yorkshireman was soon in the thick of the action when he retrieved a lost cause after Martin Hicks's header appeared to being going out of play. Somehow, Whitehurst managed to flick the ball back into the danger area, where it found Mick Tait, who tapped it home in the 23rd minute.

Millwall's equaliser after 32 minutes came when Kevin O'Callaghan's corner was insufficiently dealt with by Royals 'keeper Steve Francis's weak punch. The ball fell to former Reading man Terry Hurlock, who joyfully thumped home from 10 yards. Reading regained the lead in the 36th minute when skipper Martin Hicks drifted beyond the Millwall defence to prod home Colin Ballie's long free-kick.

With Millwall seeking promotion to the First Division for the first time, the situation required some straight talking from manager John Docherty during the interval to convince the players that they could achieve their goal. One question that he put to the players was 'did they really want to play in a higher grade of football?' If the answer was yes, then they needed to show the spirit and commitment that had been lacking recently.

Whatever Docherty said during his half-time wind-up chat certainly had the desired effect, for within five minutes of the restart a half-time deficit had been turned into a 3–2 lead and an eventual winning score. Showing renewed vigour, Millwall had Reading chasing shadows, with Irish winger Kevin O'Callaghan laying on the two goals for Teddy Sheringham.

The first cross that 'Cally' supplied saw Teddy prod home a loose ball after Royals 'keeper Steve Francis could only parry Les Briley's effort in the 46th minute. Reading had hardly recovered from that blow before they found themselves trailing in the game for the first time after 50 minutes when O'Callaghan raced on to Danis Salman's excellent through ball. His stunning centre was met by Sheringham, who dived between Reading defenders Keith Curle and Michael Gilkes to head home his 15th goal of the campaign.

This result was just the springboard that Millwall required, as they went on an unbeaten run of 12 games, which would catapult them into the First Division as champions of the Second Division.

Reading 2	Millwall 3
Tait, Hicks	Hurlock, Sheringham (2)

Reading: Francis, Baillie, Gilkes; Beavon (Madden), Hicks, Curle, Williams, Tait, Whitehurst, Moran, Smillie.
Millwall: Horne, Salman, Coleman, Stevens, Wood, McLeary, Hurlock, Briley, Sheringham, Cascarino, O'Callaghan.

35

MILLWALL V

DERBY COUNTY

3 September 1988   **First Division**
The Den, London   **Attendance: 13,040**

So finally, 103 years following their formation, Millwall had made it to the promised land of the First Division. Now they were no longer the only London club not to have played at the highest level. The stage was set, after gaining a credible 2–2 draw at Aston Villa, having held a two-goal lead at one time, for their first ever game in the top flight. It was now up to the Lions not to fluff their lines for the visit of Derby County in this historical fixture at Cold Blow Lane.

Millwall, however, may not have graced the Den with a victory had captain Les Briley not got himself off the treatment table following a very late fitness test. As always, Les led by example and, despite carrying a knock, he played with a ferocity combined with excellent distribution and, above all, inspirational leadership.

The team's combative nature, which had served them well in clinching the Second Division title earlier in the year, was again evident against the

Millwall's initial game in the First Division saw them entertain Derby County. Shown here is Tony Cascarino in the role of a Ram sandwich, he narrowly fails to connect with a centre. The game's only goal was scored by Teddy Sheringham seen here in the background.

Rams. Their England centre-half, Mark Wright, received a nasty gash above the right eye as early as the third minute. It was clearly Millwall's intention to go at Derby from the off, as Tony Cascarino and Teddy Sheringham led the barrage of attacks that threatened to overwhelm the visitors. The early bombardment should have produced two Millwall goals when both Kevin O'Callaghan and George Lawrence sprung County's fragile offside trap. It was the considerable frame of Peter Shilton that frustrated the Lions, and not for the first time, for Shilton had been a formidable obstacle on his previous visits to New Cross.

But Millwall plugged away, as efforts from Steve Wood and Cascarino flashed inches over the bar, before the goal that the Den had waited so long to see finally arrived in the 45th minute, and there was nothing that the stranded Shilton could do about it. It came about when Lawrence sent over a decent centre that found his wing partner, O'Callaghan, whose skewed shot cum cross ran parallel with the goalline, and from no more than six inches Sheringham was there to tap home.

As a delighted Sheringham ran off to celebrate, the fans roared their approval, with the hope of more to come in the second half. Millwall's stranglehold on the game was rarely tested, but goalkeeper Brian Horne earned the plaudits with a fine one-handed save from Phil Gee, with the Derby substitute probably wondering how he had missed an absolute sitter.

The final score flattered Derby, for truthfully it was a 1–0 massacre. The central defensive pairing of Wood and the immaculate Alan McLeary doused any threat offered by the Derby attack, while the midfield efforts of Briley and Terry Hurlock threw Derby completely out of kilter. Derby were outplayed and out-thought by an enterprising Millwall team that displayed an air of confidence and an abundance of skill. Derby centre-half, Mark Wright, stated, 'It was like the Alamo out there. They came at us right from the start and put us under a tremendous amount of pressure.'

Millwall 1   Derby County 0
Sheringham

Millwall: Horne, Salman, Dawes, Hurlock, Wood, McLeary, Lawrence, Briley, Sheringham, Cascarino, O'Callaghan (Carter).
Derby County: Shilton, Sage, Forsyth, Williams, Wright, Blades, Micklewhite (Pickering), Chiedozie (Gee), Goddard, Hebberd, Callaghan.

36

MILLWALL V

NORWICH CITY

22 January 1989   **First Division**
The Den, London   **Attendance: 13,687**

This gripping encounter was televised to 50 countries on five continents, but whether it was stage fright or first-night nerves, Millwall found themselves two down after seven minutes. The Lions managed to draw level, before falling to a wonder strike by Robert Fleck in the third minute of injury time.

Norwich looked the likely lads following the kick-off, as their two early strikes indicated. When Millwall's goalkeeper Brian Horne failed to deal with Dale Gordon's corner, defender Ian Butterworth reacted to drill home the loose ball for his first League goal in the second minute. The Lions 'keeper was again at fault five minutes later when he allowed Andy Linighan's drive to slip from his grasp, leaving Fleck and Robert Rosario to set up full-back Mark Bowen to add the second goal from close range.

The humiliation that Millwall were facing ended as abruptly as it started, when two of the Lions' Irish contingent combined to reduce the lead in the 11th minute, with Tony Cascarino's sublime finish the result of Kevin

Millwall's excellent left-back Ian Dawes and Norwich City's Dale Gordon, who himself joined the Lions a few years later, seen vying for possession in what was one of The Den's greatest matches.

Two Irish internationals battle for possession at The Den, which sees Millwall's Kevin O'Callaghan outwit Andy Townsend of Norwich.

O'Callaghan's excellent run and cross. From that moment on, Millwall battered Norwich, but not before Horne redeemed himself with a flying save from an Andy Townsend piledriver.

Down at the other end, Bryan Gunn began to distinguish himself in the Norwich goal by tipping over O'Callaghan's header and then Jimmy Carter's tantalising cross. Despite the buffeting they received, City seemed to be heading into the break ahead, but when Ian Dawes and Terry Hurlock instigated a terrific build-up down the left, the equaliser looked imminent. The move was continued by Teddy Sheringham and Darren Morgan, in for the suspended skipper Les Briley. The superb exchange of passes put Morgan into a threatening position within the Norwich area. His square pass was ideally weighted for the onrushing Carter to blast home the equaliser in the 42nd minute.

The second half was nearly all one-way traffic as Norwich came under increasing pressure. Gunn denied Cascarino twice, and O'Callaghan and Sheringham once. His best moment was when he instinctively blocked Cascarino's close-range volley and had the crowd gasping disbelievingly.

A Norwich response came after 76 minutes, when Gordon's crisp left-foot shot brought a spectacular save from Horne. With the crowd still roaring them on, the bets were on Millwall winning, but deep into stoppage time, a Norwich break saw Danis Salman wearily place his clearance in the one spot that it should not have gone. As it dropped, the waiting Fleck saw his stunning volley, his first goal for 12 weeks, fly past a startled Horne from the edge of the area to win the game.

Millwall 2	Norwich City 3
Cascarino, Carter	Butterworth, Bowen, Fleck

Millwall: Horne, Salman, Dawes, Hurlock, Wood, McLeary, Carter, Morgan, Sheringham, Cascarino, O'Callaghan.
Norwich City: Gunn, Culverhouse, Linighan, Butterworth, Bowen, Gordon, Phelan, Townsend, Putney, Rosario, Fleck.

Terry Hurlock, Darren Morgan [on ground] and Andy Townsend illustrate what a midfield battle looks like, while Robert Fleck of Norwich City is merely an onlooker.

37

MILLWALL V

ASTON VILLA

16 December 1989　　　　　　　　　　**First Division**
The Den, London　　　　　　　　**Attendance: 10,536**

Millwall's reluctance to splash the cash during the close season was to come back to haunt them long before the end of their second season in the top flight. Manager John Docherty's reliance on the players who had served him so well the previous year, when the Lions finished in a more than respectful 10th place, was not only misplaced, but totally negligent. By all accounts, and according to the late chairman Reg Burr, money was available to strengthen the squad, but Doc's hesitancy in the transfer market would ultimately cost him his job, and he was relieved of his duties in February 1990.

So this fixture against Aston Villa represented something of landmark for Millwall, as it would be their fifth and last victory obtained in the old First Division. With no victories in the last 10 matches, the Lions needed to start winning, and quickly. For Villa, chasing Championship honours, two points looked like easy pickings after attaining the third spot in the table following eight wins from 10 matches.

Official Programme £1

Lewisham

THE LIONS

BARCLAYS LEAGUE
DIVISION ONE

ASTON VILLA

SATURDAY
16th DECEMBER 1989
KICK-OFF 3.00 p.m.

Lions star Keith Stevens roars out some encouragement to his team-mates.

SPALL

The bringing together of Terry Hurlock and skipper Les Briley into Millwall's midfield for the first time in five matches certainly galvanised the Lions, as their absence through suspension and injury had seen Millwall slip from seventh place down to 17th.

Villa's rise up the table was in no small way down to the craft and skill of Gordon Cowans and David Platt, but Millwall's resurgent midfield stifled them both, so much so that the threats of Tony Daley on the flanks and Ian Olney through the middle were nullified. The importance of Briley and Hurlock to Millwall was shown continually as they chipped away at Villa's resolve in a game where chances were at a premium.

Not allowing Villa time to settle suited Millwall in their current predicament, and soon after the kick-off the Lions declared their intentions when Jimmy Carter fired across the Villa goal, before Hurlock waded through three crunching tackles, only to fire high over Nigel Spink's crossbar.

So, following a goalless first half, in which Millwall's aerial bombardment failed to breach Paul McGrath and Derek Mountfield's solid defence, it came as a surprise when Villa's duo were undone four minutes after the break. Jimmy Carter found some rare space down the left to plant his cross for Tony Cascarino to head home unhindered at the far post. Villa hit back with their first meaningful attack five minutes later when a subdued Platt prepared to shoot, but was foiled by Briley's excellent tackle.

Millwall began fading a little, but the energetic and unflagging pairing of Briley and Hurlock brought a spring back into the team's step when they engineered Millwall's second goal after 63 minutes. Gaining a free-kick just outside the Villa penalty area, Briley left it to Hurlock to thunder his effort into Villa's defensive wall. But Cowan's attempted clearance went straight to Briley, who promptly switched the ball for Paul Stephenson to slide the ball past Spink from a narrow angle.

With 15 minutes to go, Villa finally gave Millwall 'keeper Brian Horne some action to deal with. An excellent run and cross from Chris Price saw Horne go down to save Paul McGrath's header. Villa's best football came in the last 10 minutes, but by then it was all too late, although there still time for Platt to carve out a goal attempt that forced an equally fine save from Horne in the 87th minute.

Despite the win, the Lions's fortunes plummeted further still with the departure of Tony Cascarino for a £1.5 million fee to Aston Villa in March. The money received allowed two new additions to the squad, but internationals Malcolm Allen of Wales and Ireland's Mick McCarthy came too late to halt Millwall's descent back to the Second Division; Villa finished runners-up to Liverpool.

Millwall 2   Aston Villa 0
Cascarino, Stephenson

Millwall: Horne, Stevens, Dawes, Briley, Thompson, McLeary, Carter, Hurlock, Torpey, Cascarino, Stephenson.
Aston Villa: Spink, Price, Gray (Williams), McGrath, Mountfield, Nielsen (Blake), Daley, Platt, Olney, Cowan, Ormondroyd.

38

MILLWALL V

NOTTS COUNTY

19 September 1992   **Second Division**
The Den, London   **Attendance: 6,689**

With goalless draws in three of their last four fixtures, Millwall had been threatening to give one opponent a severe thrashing before too long, and the unfortunate victims happened to be Neil Warnock's Notts County.

But one manager's nightmare is another's dream, and Millwall boss Mick McCarthy could not have wished for anything better than six goals, a clean sheet and a standing ovation from an appreciative home support. County were decimated by injuries, and had also recently sold Craig Short for £2.5 million and replaced him with centre-back Dave Robinson from Peterborough, who was making his debut. Nonetheless, County, having won their two previous away matches, could have taken the lead when Sidcup-born Dave Smith attempted a goal, but he missed horribly. The visitors' vulnerability down the flanks was exposed when Millwall took the lead in the 17th minute. Kenny Cunningham's run and pinpoint cross was nodded down by the outstanding 18-year-old Andy Roberts for Jon Goodman to sweep home.

Millwall's Colin Cooper was converted from a decent left-back into a superb centre-back at The Den, and following his transfer to Nottingham Forest, he later went on to play for England. Colin is seen here keeping tabs on Notts County's Kevin Wilson.

After going without goal in the previous four games, Millwall certainly went to town when thumping Notts County in the last season at Cold Blow Lane. Phil Barber is seen celebrating one of his two goals and is congratulated by Malcolm Allen [left] and Tony Dolby [centre].

As the Lions' confidence grew, so did their dominance, although County issued a timely statement when Kevin Wilson forced Kasey Keller into a smart save, before Dean Thomas skimmed the Millwall crossbar with a blistering 25-yard blast.

But, sadly for County, such efforts were few and far between, as it left Millwall with a stranglehold on proceedings for most of the second-half. The catalyst for County's sufferings was the return of the Lions' Welsh international, Malcolm Allen. Back from a three-game suspension, Allen turned what appeared to be a close-run contest into a rout. The Welsh-speaking player was at his bewitching best and helped Millwall to register three goals in four minutes. The second goal saw him dummy new boy Robinson to calmly slot the ball into the corner of the net after 54 minutes.

A minute later, a determined Phil Barber scored the third after shrugging off a couple of half-hearted challenges. The game was up for a dejected County after conceding a fourth in the 55th minute. Millwall's fourth goal followed some excellent build-up play between Ian Dawes and Allen, which left Barber to finish off a scintillating move. Further distress was heaped on County when Shaun Murphy's mind wandered off elsewhere to allow Allen to score goal number five in the 70th minute.

Millwall then had a couple of decent penalty shouts waved away by the referee, Peter Foakes, who had obviously taken pity on the hapless visitors. The first occurred when Allen was bundled over in the area by Robinson. Phil Barber was then denied a hat-trick when Phil Turner was seen to punch his header off the line. But Millwall's joy was complete two minutes from time with a sixth goal, thanks again to Allen. With some superb artistry following a weak County clearance, Allen rode an equally flimsy challenge to lay it on a plate for Tony Dolby to tap in.

The defeat left County manager agonising over his future at Meadow Lane, but he offered no excuses for his team's lamentable second-half showing, although defender Robinson protested, 'You couldn't just blame the defence. There were shortcomings all over the field. It's easy to say that we had a lot of players out through injury, but there's so much depth in the squad that it should have prevented a catastrophe like that.'

In contrast, the Millwall dressing room was full of smiling faces, with five-star performances all round, especially from 18-year-olds Tony Dolby, who was making his first full start, and Andy Roberts.

Millwall 6   Notts County 0
Allen (2), Barber (2),
Goodman, Dolby

Millwall: Keller, Cunningham, Dawes, May (Holsgrove), Cooper, Stevens, Roberts, Dolby, Goodman (McGinlay), Barber.
Notts County: Cherry, Djkstra, Thomas, Murphy, Robinson, O'Riordan, Draper, Turner, Lund, Wilson (Slawson), Smith.

39

MILLWALL V BRISTOL ROVERS

8 May 1993
The Den, London

Second Division
Attendance: 15,821

It was the end of an era for Millwall; the time had come for the Lions to say a fond farewell to the Den, which had been their home for the last 83 years.

Having failed to qualify for play-offs by finishing seventh, the game against relegated Bristol Rovers should have been pressure free, in a final celebration of one of England's most atmospheric and sometimes notorious stadiums. Instead, the supporters were treated to a limp and insipid display.

It is hard to pick the bones out of this showing, as Rovers, already preparing for life in the Third Division, took the lead in the 35th minute. The move started from Billy Clark's throw-in, which was worked across the width of the pitch by Marcus Stewart and John Taylor to pave the way for the speedy Lee Archer to fire clinically into the bottom of the net. Despite putting Rovers under some early pressure, Millwall never looked likely to end their years at the Den victorious.

MILLWALL 50 GREATEST MATCHES

Any thoughts about a fightback by the Lions were snuffed out within seconds of the restart when the visitors increased their lead. Stewart must have thought that it was a training match when sprinting through a static Millwall defence onto Justin Channing's through ball. As Lions 'keeper Kasey Keller advanced to narrow the angle, Stewart nonchalantly slipped the ball into the net. The goal killed off Millwall; even the award of a penalty in the 68th minute failed to reignite their flame.

In keeping with their tepid performance, Malcolm Allen's spot-kick was saved by Rovers 'keeper Brian Parkin. Ten minutes later the first pitch invasion occurred, and even that seemed half-hearted. When order had been restored, Bristol went further ahead after 80 minutes when 18-year-old Mike Davis, who had only been signed from Yate Town a fortnight earlier, dispossessed Gavin Maguire some 40 yards out – striding forward with purpose and composure to side-foot inside Keller's left-hand post for goal number three.

The Lions were finally put out of their misery in a very sad finale. After the teams left the ground for the last time, it was left to the souvenir hunters to commence the demolition work at Cold Blow Lane.

Millwall 0   Bristol Rovers 3
                       Archer, Stewart, Davis

Millwall: Keller, Dawes, Cooper, Maguire, Manning (Dolby), Barber, Roberts, Rae, Allen, Moralee (Verveer).
Bristol Rovers: Parkin, Clark, Tilson, Yates, Maddison, Mehew (Reece), Channing, Waddock, Archer, Stewart (Davis), Taylor.

40

WIGAN ATHLETIC V MILLWALL

17 May 2000
JJB Stadium, Wigan

Third Division Play-off
Semi-final Second Leg
Attendance: 10,642

Having been held to a 0–0 draw in the first leg, Millwall would have to pull out all the stops if they were to make a second visit to Wembley Stadium in little over a year a reality. Both teams remained unchanged from the first game, and at the end of 90 minutes Millwall were left scratching their heads, wondering how they lost such a compelling game.

Following on from Saturday's drab meeting, one goal either way was always going to settle the tie, and so it was. Even so, Darren Sheridan's 61st-minute winner from a free-kick was laced with a slice of good fortune: fate seemed to intervene when David Livermore inadvertently diverted the ball past Tony Warner, when the goalkeeper appeared to have set himself for a straightforward save.

The goal was not Sheridan's only contribution over the two games. It was he who denied Paul Moody a goal in the first match, and was again in the thick of the action two minutes after scoring the decisive strike. Tim

wigan athletic official matchday programme
wednesday 17th may 2000 kick off 7.45pm
versus **millwall**
number 30 . price £2.00
nationwide league division two
play-off semi final second leg

new kit launched tonight

Nationwide
FOOTBALL LEAGUE

MILLWALL FC

Main Club sponsor

JJB SPORTS

Kit sponsor

adidas

Drinks sponsor

LUCOZADE SPORT

YEAR OF PROMISE
itv

Executive Match Sponsor
Diadora (UK) Ltd

Match Ball Sponsor
Umbro Sports Drink

Match Programme Sponsor
Alan Jolley Design Services

Cahill's far-post header looked to have brought the teams level, but up popped Sheridan to whack the ball clear. These three acts were to determine who would face Gillingham in the Play-off Final.

It was a night of frustration at Wigan and this photo shows goalkeeper Tony Warner and left-back Robbie Ryan halting another Latics attack.

If chances counted then Millwall would have been home and dry long before the end, with their best opportunity of the first half being Lucas Neill's effort in the 27th minute; his swerving free-kick forced Wigan 'keeper Derek Stillie into a drastic clearance. While at the other end, Neil Redfearn's effort

The quicksilver pace of Lion Paul Ifill is momentarily halted by the arm of a Wigan defender in the play-off semi-final.

was deflected just around a post, before Matt Lawrence spirited away Simon Haworth's dangerous cross before it reached Andy Liddell.

The second half was barely 10 minutes old when Cahill saw another splendid effort turned away in the 53rd minute, and then five minutes later he beat Stillie, only to see his strike deflect off Pat McGibbon after his goalkeeper spilled a cross from Neil Harris. After Wigan's fortuitous goal, it was Millwall who played the tune for the last third of the game.

Two flashing headers from Paul Moody went agonisingly close, with Millwall's most potent attacker of the night, Neil Harris, bringing another fine save from Stillie. The Wigan 'keeper reacted even better 10 minutes from time when teammate Scott Green's wayward header seemed destined for the top corner of the net, but Stillie went at full stretch to keep it out. Eventually, time and luck ran out for the Lions. Latics manager John Benson's post-match comment summed up the game perfectly when he said, 'It's no use kidding ourselves, the back three won it'.

Wigan Athletic 1   Millwall 0
Sheridan

Wigan Athletic: Stillie, McGibbon, Balmer, De Zeeuw, Green, Redfearn, Sheridan, Kilford, Sharp, Haworth, Liddell.
Millwall: Warner, Lawrence, Nethercott, Tuttle, Ryan (Shaw), Ifill, Cahill, Livermore, Neill (Kinet), Moody Harris.

41

WREXHAM V MILLWALL

28 April 2001   **Second Division**
Racecourse Ground, Wrexham   **Attendance: 5,939**

So the Lions eventually got the draw they needed to acquire promotion when the game finally ended at around 5.20pm, following two interruptions. The match had barely been in play for two minutes when 200 Millwall fans without tickets were ushered into an already fully-subscribed away end. Having spilled on to the pitch, the fans caused the game to be held up for 23 minutes while referee Mark Cowburn took both the teams off.

When play recommenced, Millwall were hard-pressed to make any inroads against Wrexham after Craig Faulconbridge had volleyed them ahead after just nine minutes. Falling behind so early left them with a very steep hill to climb, and the rain lashing down did not help either.

Millwall foraged hard to draw level, and two attempts involved Dave Livermore. The former Arsenal trainee fired in one effort, which Tim Cahill was quick to follow up, but the Welshman cleared the danger. Then Livermore, with only goalkeeper Dave Walsh to beat, missed the target altogether. In a poor first half, the visitors' only other decent effort was

home the equaliser...

Millwall obtained the point they needed to gain promotion in 2001 and this fine action shot shows Lions striker Paul Moody attempting to unsettle the Wrexham defence. The ball finally reached Tim Cahill who headed home a dramatic equaliser.

Cahill's volley, which was expertly dealt with by Walsh. A Lee Trundle shot and an effort from Darren Ferguson caused some flutter among the travelling support, but Tony Warner was equal to both. The Racecourse has not been a happy hunting ground for Millwall and, with events looking a tad precarious, half-time could not come quick enough.

The sun broke through at the start of the second half, and was shining on Millwall's fortunes when they equalised in the 53rd minute. Millwall gained a corner, which Livermore took to find the leaping Tim Cahill, who crashed home a header for his 10th and most vital goal of the season. After the match, Cahill proudly said, 'This goal is a landmark for me. It's taken me into double figures for the season.' The goal brought the fans back on to the field, but fortunately it was just for a couple minutes this time, although it did not stop the referee announcing that if there were any more encroachments, he would not hesitate to abandon the game.

The post-match celebrations are underway at the Racecourse ground and leading the way are midfielder Marc Bircham and goalkeeper Tony Warner along with a couple of fans.

Late in the game, Millwall became more of a force as they went in search of a winner and nearly obtained it on a couple of occasions. Neil Harris's fierce shot was turned around the post by the ever-alert Walsh. Then the Welsh Under-21 'keeper denied Christoph Kinet, but required the help of teammate Danny Williams, who cleared Livermore's goal-bound strike off the line.

As the game drifted towards a conclusion, news filtered through that Reading had lost at Colchester. This result would confirm that a point would be enough for Millwall to clinch promotion. Elevation was assured by the final whistle, which came some 25 minutes after every other game had finished. This match would define Millwall's Championship-winning campaign.

Wrexham 1   Millwall 1
Faulconbridge   Cahill

Wrexham: Walsh, Hardy, McGregor, Carey, Ridley, Edwards (Gibson), Williams, Ferguson, Trundle, Faulconbridge, Russell.
Millwall: Warner, Neill (Bircham), Nethercott, Dyche, Lawrence, Reid, Livermore, Cahill, Ifill (Kinet), Claridge (Moody), Harris.

42

MILLWALL V

COVENTRY CITY

3 November 2001   **First Division**
The Den, London   **Attendance: 15,748**

Millwall's momentum following promotion in April was still evident after a third of the Championship fixtures had been completed, and in this win over Coventry City their energy levels appeared inexhaustible. But for the fans, having watched a pedestrian first 45 minutes, the word 'energy' would not spring immediately to mind, as the half ended, predictably, 0–0.

It was City who looked likely to score in a drab first half, when Lee Hughes cottoned on to Delorge's pass to force Lions goalkeeper Tony Warner to turn his drive round the post after 27 minutes. Then, four minutes before the break, Jay Bothroyd, a substitute for the ailing Hughes, found Jairo Martinez outpacing the Lions defence, only to see Warner turn his effort over the bar.

The situation had to change, and it did, dramatically. Millwall manager Mark McGhee altered his formation from 3–5–2, back to the tried-and-tested 4–4–2 for the start of the second half. McGhee's tweaking came to fruition in the 55th minute, when the indefatigable Steve Claridge volleyed

After a fairly mundane first-half game against Coventry City, the game exploded into an end-to-end contest, Steve Claridge is seen turning away after giving Millwall the lead in the 55th minute.

home with Millwall's first meaningful shot on target after Coventry failed to clear a Kinet corner.

Going a goal behind stung City into action, and they were back level on the hour when Honduran Martinez forced home David Thompson's corner. Eight minutes later they went in front, after Bothroyd, who since coming on had become a constant menace to the Millwall defence, scored with a finely struck drive into the corner of Warner's net from 25 yards. The pacey Martinez then got through again, but could only watch as his effort roll across the face of an unguarded goal.

These City efforts set the crowd going as Millwall pushed forward in search of a goal, and when City captain Gary Breen grabbed Claridge on the edge of the area, it gave the Lions an opportunity. With only 10 minutes left, in true Beckham style Millwall's Belgian left-winger, Christophe Kinet, curled his exquisite effort around the Coventry wall and in.

Their tails firmly up, Millwall poured forward in search of a winner. A flashpoint occurred involving the battling Thompson in the 87th minute; he clattered Paul Ifill, not once, but twice, leaving referee Keith Hill no option but to dish out a red card. Instead of shutting up shop, City also went in search of the decisive goal, but were caught on the break by the inspirational veteran Claridge. On approaching the angle of the City penalty area, Claridge delicately scooped up a cross that goalkeeper Marcus Hedman could only flap at. The half-clearance fell conveniently on to the head of Lions skipper Stuart Nethercott, who sent the ball back across goal for the stooping Richard Sadlier to place his header in at the far post. The winner brought the house down and sewed up a stirring victory in the last minute.

This was indeed a game of two halves, and following Coventry's defeat, their first in 12 games, Millwall could count themselves fortunate in claiming all three points.

Millwall 3   Coventry City 2
Claridge, Kinet,   Martinez, Bothroyd
Sadlier

Millwall: Warner, Green, Nethercott, Ward (Kinet, Ryan), Dyche, Bull, Ifill, Cahill, Livermore, Claridge, Sadlier.
Coventry City: Hedman, Edworthy, Shaw, Safri, Konjic, Breen, Thompson, Carsley, Hughes (Bothroyd), Martinez, Delorge.

43

MILLWALL V

PORTSMOUTH

1 March 2003   **First Division**
The Den, London   **Attendance: 9,697**

Following a couple of exceptional campaigns, the Lions found the 2002–03 season one of fluctuating fortunes. There had been some impressive victories, such as beating Coventry away 3–2, and the demolition of Watford at the Den 4–0. These successes were intermingled with some desperate early home losses – to Rotherham 6–0 and Walsall 3–0. These defeats would be the precursor of things to come throughout a frustrating season.

By the time that Pompey arrived in SE16, they were League leaders and looked like certainties for the Premier League. As embarrassments go, the Walsall and Rotherham games took some beating. This encounter was hardly any less embarrassing, and this was down to one man.

The player concerned was Pompey captain Paul Merson, who gave a virtuoso performance with his pristine passing and his unique ability to spot an opening. This potent mix was just too much for the Lions, as the magical Merson weaved his spell to destroy Millwall with an overwhelming and influential performance.

One of the best talents to come out of Millwall was Steven Reid who was later capped by the Republic of Ireland. Steven is pictured here showing a clean pair to heels to Portsmouth's Tim Sherwood.

The carnage began in the 15th minute, when Yukubu drilled home a low drive, not long after Millwall had spurned the chance to open the scoring when young defender Paul Robinson failed to make proper contact with a header. If Portsmouth's goal had been against the run of play, their next goal put them in control, which they never looked like relinquishing.

Bulgarian Svetoslav Todorov, who in the 23rd minute had been foiled by Lions 'keeper Tony Warner, again confronted the home custodian a minute later. But on this occasion he squared the ball for Yakubu to stroke home for the second. Millwall responded through a Neil Harris volley from the edge of the six-yard box, which went too high, before Steve Claridge failed to get clean contact on David Livermore's knock-down.

Pompey's third goal came through another flaw in Millwall's defensive policy when Kevin Harper exploited the acres of space afforded him on the right to hit a cross for Tim Sherwood to rise unchallenged and head over Warner after 31 minutes. When Todorov added the fourth from another Merson pass on the stroke of half-time, the home fans feared that another drubbing was on the cards. To their eternal credit, Millwall did not capitulate, and soon after the restart Robbie Ryan saw his 20-yard rocket tipped over by the diving Shaka Hislop.

Compared to the many chances Millwall had created in the second period, Pompey's chances came at a premium. They scored with one and thumped the other against crossbar. Millwall's spirited response was probably down to the haranguing the team got from manager Mark McGhee at the break. Their best effort came when Christoph Kinet's stunning free-kick appeared to be heading for the net, but somehow Hislop's leap to his right kept the ball out. The giant Portsmouth goalkeeper was also equal to a couple of Paul Ifill's long-range specials.

Pompey and the unplayable Merson were not finished just yet, however, and when Robinson flattened Yukubu in the area, the former Arsenal man fired home the fifth from the penalty spot with 18 minutes left. A sixth Portsmouth goal was denied when the resilient Warner spread himself to block Nigel Quashie's effort. Paul Merson's masterclass came to an end when he was substituted after 81 minutes by Diabate. As Merson departed the scene of his triumph, the crowd rose as one to applaud him back to the bench in appreciation of a very talented footballer. Afterwards, Merson expressed his gratitude, 'I was touched by the ovation; it's not something that happens to visiting players here. I knew they meant it. They are real fans. This carries more weight because of where I was.'

Millwall 0   Portsmouth 5
                              Yakubu (2), Sherwood, Todorov, Merson (pen)

Millwall: Warner, Reid, Robinson, Ward, Ryan, Kinet, Ifill, Wise, Livermore, Harris, Claridge (Sadlier).
Portsmouth: Hislop, Harper (Crowe), Primus, De Zeeuw, Festa, Taylor, Sherwood, Quashie, Merson (Diabate), Todorov (Pericard), Aiyebeni.

44

MILLWALL V WEST HAM UNITED

21 March 2004 **First Division**
The Den, London **Attendance: 14.055**

This match will go down in the annals of Millwall Football Club as the Mother's Day massacre in which they nearly equalled and surpassed their biggest winning margin over the Hammers (5–1 in March 1912).

Millwall's emphatic win brought them within a point of West Ham, with only one goal keeping them out of the top six play-off places. The game, however, was incident packed, with three penalties, a red card and quite a few disaffected Hammers fans. The Hammers' failure to combat the windy conditions saw them fall behind in the 34th minute. Winger Paul Ifill took advantage of the space in front of him down the left, then whipped in a cross that isolated West Ham goalkeeper Stephen Bywater. In his attempt to clear the danger, Hammers skipper Christian Dailly could only divert the ball into the corner of his own goal.

Millwall should have been ahead earlier when Matt Etherington tripped Ifill in the area, but Neil Harris's poor penalty-kick hit Bywater's legs and was scrambled clear. West Ham's response was a 30-yard dipping volley

The final nail in the Hammer's coffin in the 'Mother's Day Massacre' fixture sees on loan Everton striker Nick Chadwick thrash home Millwall's fourth goal.

Mob-handed: Millwall's Danny Dichio, Matt Lawrence Kevin Muscat Darren ward Andy Roberts and Robbie Ryan celebrate the third goal against West Ham. While Paul Ifill [provider] and Tim Cahill [scorer] enjoy one another's company.

from Kevin Horlock that was tipped over by Lions 'keeper Andy Marshall. But the real action was reserved for the second half, which had been in progress barely a minute when Everton loanee Nick Chadwick, a half-time substitute for Danny Dichio, sent over delightful cross for Tim Cahill to rise unchallenged and head home for the second.

West Ham reduced the lead in the 49th minute when Matt Lawrence, for reasons best known to himself, handled Horlock's free-kick in the area. The only successful penalty of the afternoon came when Marlon Harewood stroked home by sending Marshall the wrong way. There was more panic in the Hammers defence, which nearly led to Millwall increasing their lead, when Bywater's fly kick rebounded off Harris, only for the ball to roll agonisingly wide of an open goal.

West Ham's respite was brief, however, after a minor spat between Tomas Repka and Cahill resulted in a corner for Millwall, and Cahill, with acres of room, thumped a stunning left-foot effort into the roof of the net. There was more drama on the hour when Harris sprung the offside trap, and in the process of lobbing Bywater, Harris was checked by the Hammers 'keeper, who was red-carded by referee Jeff Winters for his troubles.

Here was the chance for the Australian Cahill to claim his first Millwall hat-trick, but to the amazement of the Millwall faithful he blasted the ball high into the south stand. A rare West Ham attack saw substitute Brian Deane have his short-range effort smothered by the alert Marshall to preserve Millwall's lead. Some indolent defending by the Czech international, Repka, was rightly punished when Cahill's forward punt dropped for Chadwick to belt his shot high into the net for the fourth goal in the 79th minute.

Millwall 4	West Ham United 1
Dailly (og),	Harewood (pen)
Cahill (2),	
Chadwick	

Millwall: Marshall, Muscat, Lawrence, Ward, Ryan, Ifill, Roberts, Cahill, Livermore, Harris, Dichio (Chadwick).

West Ham United: Bywater, Repka, Dailly, Melville, Harley, Reo-Coker, Carrick, Horlock (Deane), Etherington (Srnicek), Zamora, Harewood (McAnuff).

45

SUNDERLAND V MILLWALL

4 April 2004
Old Trafford, Manchester

FA Cup Semi-final
Attendance: 56,112

This was Millwall's first appearance in the semi-final since that groundbreaking day in 1937 when the Lions became the first Third Division club to reach such a stage and, as fate would decree, they would face the same opponent in this match – Sunderland.

But 67 years later there was a lot more familiarity between the teams, Millwall having already completed the double over the Black Cats. Adding to an already spicy encounter was the fact that the man in charge at the Stadium of Light was none other than the former Millwall player and manager, Mick McCarthy.

The spice on the pitch would come from the likes of Millwall's player-manager Dennis Wise and his captain, Kevin Muscat, while Sunderland could offer Jason McAteer, Paul Thirlwell and George McCartney, and it was no surprise that four of these combatants picked up bookings.

Millwall negotiated a sticky and nervous opening that began in earnest after six minutes when Julio Arca's free-kick rattled the underside of the bar, with

Millwall's Australian international Tim Cahill had a penchant for scoring vital goals and none more important than the one against Sunderland in the FA Cup semi-final at Old Trafford.

Andy Marshall beaten before the danger was cleared. Millwall's nerves started to fray with more Sunderland pressure; a Tommy Smith knock-down presented John Oster with an excellent chance, but groans from the Black Cats' fans were audible when he put his effort high over the bar.

Finally, through Neil Harris, Millwall got going when the Lions' talisman evaded a couple of lunging tackles; but alas, there no one available to take advantage of his cross. Another Millwall advance was halted when Neil ran on to Paul Ifill's through ball after he was challenged by two Sunderland defenders. The Black Cats' response was another wild blast from McAteer, who launched Oster's pass into orbit.

In 1937 Millwall took an early lead, and something similar happened in this match in the 25th minute, and it would see the Lions march into the record books. When George McCartney hit his woefully short back pass to former Lion Phil Babb, it gave Ifill the opportunity to nip in and steal the ball from under Babb's nose. Swooping in on Mart Poom's goal, the flying winger rounded a covering defender. Feinting to shoot, Ifill shimmied again, then hit the ball hard and true, only for Poom to block miraculously.

As the ball came to Millwall's latest international, the Australian Tim Cahill, his mid-air twist defied logic as he drilled the ball over a group of players and high into Poom's goal. Wheeling away in delight, Tim raced along to where the Millwall fans were congregated, swirling his shirt triumphantly above his head.

The tackles from a piqued Sunderland team began to bite, with Ifill becoming the first victim, whose crime was having the temerity to create the goal, and he was stretchered off in the 27th minute. Kevin Muscat, who, by his own standards, had a quiet game, went off by the same mode of transport 12 minutes later – the victim of McAteer's horrendous tackle.

These injuries failed to rattle Millwall, who not only kept their shape but also their belief. Even the threat of Kevin Kyle, the Sunderland striker, failed to upset their composure, although he managed some disquiet with a header and then a shot. The Lions centre-back duo, the rugged Matt Lawrence and the immaculate Darren Ward, held firm throughout, without having to resort to any strong-arm measures.

Although Arca and Thirlwell had efforts on the Millwall goal, neither threatened, but Marshall had to be at his very best to deny Kyle's powerful

It's the Millennium and Europe here we come, as members of the squad are enjoying themselves as they soak up the atmosphere following the victory over the Makems.

header. This was to be Kyle's last meaningful contribution, however, and a pleasing sight for the Millwall contingent was to see the big Scot surprisingly hauled off by Mick McCarthy on the hour. As former Sunderland striker Niall Quinn said after the game, 'When Kyle came off the pitch the defenders would have gone, "Woah, thank God he's gone!"'

Down at the other end, Harris combined with Danny Dichio to tee up David Livermore, whose drive went skew-whiff, before Millwall nearly settled the tie with 16 minutes to go. Cahill got away down the right to find Dichio steaming in to power in a header that was destined for the net, until Poom made a superb stop and the ball ran loose to Harris, whose follow-up struck a part of Cahill's anatomy, and the opportunity was lost.

This miss and the introduction of Matt Piper by the Black Cats heightened the anxiety, and when McCartney gained possession with only Marshall to beat, the feeling of relief in the Millwall sections of Old Trafford was audible when the Irishman screwed his effort wide. With this, Sunderland's hopes of reaching their fifth FA Cup Final had all but gone. The Black Cats' day worsened in the 85th minute when Harris was on track to make the game safe, only to be cynically hauled back by McAteer. Without waiting for referee Paul Durkin to wield a second yellow card, the shamed belligerent was last seen heading down the tunnel.

So Millwall had finally reached their first FA Cup Final after 116 years of trying. Winning it would be irrelevant; the Millwall fans were going to enjoy the occasion, no matter what the result.

Sunderland 0   Millwall 1
                      Cahill

Sunderland: Poom, Wright (Thornton), Babb (Piper), Breen, McCartney, Oster, McAteer, Arca, Thirlwell, Kyle (Stewart), Smith.
Millwall: Marshall, Muscat (Roberts), Lawrence, Ward, Ryan (Elliott), Ifill (Sweeney), Wise, Livermore, Cahill, Harris, Dichio.

46

MILLWALL V

FERENCVAROS

16 September 2004   UEFA Cup First Round First Leg
The Den, London   Attendance: 11,667

The Lions' first venture into European football was the culmination of seven of the most eventful years in the history of Millwall Football Club under the chairmanship of Theo Paphitis.

As it turned out, Millwall should have taken a substantial lead over Budapest as they dominated the match, with the vastly experienced player-manager Dennis Wise running the show from his midfield patch. The spiky Wise opened the scoring for Millwall midway in the second half when he curled home a 25-yard free-kick in the 66th minute after Stefan Moore had been body-checked by Dragan Vukmir. The goal certainly relieved the frustration felt by fans and players alike brought on by the Hungarian champions' spoiling tactics and the many opportunities missed by the Lions.

Millwall's failure to take the various chances that came along was annoying, but more annoying was to concede a goal from a free-kick given for Aleksander Bajevski's dramatic fall from David Livermore's innocuous tackle 12 minutes from time. The visitors' captain, Peter Lipcsei, was to

The front cover from the match programme versus Ferencvaros for Millwall's first adventure in Europe.

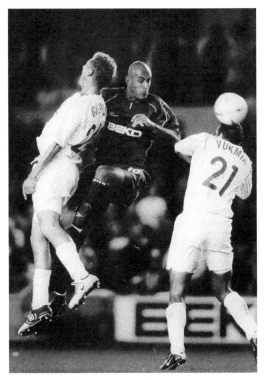

Bustling Lion; Danny Dichio gets in between two Ferencvaros defenders to power in a header.

spoil the party by crashing home the equaliser, to which Lions 'keeper Graham Stack got a hand to but could not keep out.

It was Ferencvaros, however, who created the first scare of the evening when Bajevski's effort inside the Millwall area was blocked by Darren Ward. But Millwall hit back almost immediately when Marvin Elliott's goal-bound header from a Wise corner was acrobatically tipped over by Lajos Szucs in the sixth minute. Elliott was again involved when winning a free-kick some 25 yards out, but frustratingly Neil Harris could not capitalise on Wise's exquisite chip over the Ferencvaros wall.

Again Elliott was at the fore when his long-range effort was tipped over for a corner following a Josh Simpson cross, and when Szucs flapped at another centre, Moore was slow

Millwall's Canadian international Josh Simpson feels the full weight of a Hungarian tackle at The Den in September 2004.

Jubilant team-mates surround player-manager Dennis Wise after he had opened the scoring against Ferencvaros in what was Millwall's first tilt at European football.

to react. Late in the first half, the Hungarians forced three corners, but were unable to make any of them count. Unbelievably, Ferencvaros were still on terms at the break.

Millwall commenced the second half in possession, which saw Barry Cogan elect to shoot when the Irish teenager should have set up the better-placed Harris or

Moore. The Hungarians hit back after 54 minutes with a free-kick from Daniel Toszer that ploughed into the side netting. The promising Marvin Elliott must have wondered what he had to do to score, and he was denied once more when Szucs pulled off his best save of the night to stop Millwall from going ahead once more.

The game finished in a draw and Millwall could be justifiably proud, but the majority of the observers felt that Millwall's chance of progressing to the next round had gone – and so it would prove after the 3–1 defeat in the second leg in the Hungarian capital.

The ups and downs of Millwall's journey to Europe created a rollercoaster of emotions for the team and their supporters. It is a story that few clubs of similar standing could aspire to in a generation, let alone in a period of less than a decade.

Millwall 1   Ferencvaros 1
Wise   Lipcsei

Millwall: Stack, Muscat, Lawrence, Ward, Simpson, Wise, Elliott, Livermore, Morris (Cogan), Moore (Ifill), Harris (Dichio).
Ferencvaros: Szucs, Vukmir, Gyepes, Botis, Balog (Zavadsky), Kapic, Rosa, Tozser, Lipcsei, Vagner (Penska), Bajevski (Sowumni).

47

LEEDS UNITED V MILLWALL

14 May 2009
Elland Road, Leeds

League One Play-off
Semi-final Second Leg
Attendance: 37,036

Millwall reached their first Play-off Final at the fifth attempt, after overcoming favourites Leeds United in front of a baying Yorkshire crowd, who were hoping that their team could overturn the 1–0 deficit that the Lions had inflicted upon them at the Den five days earlier.

The first flashpoint to raise the temperature even higher came after 76 seconds, when Adam Bolder clattered into United's playmaker Robert Snodgrass to earn the first yellow card of nine that referee Mark Halsey would issue during the match.

When the game finally settled down after a boisterous start, Leeds, as expected, had most of the possession, but found Millwall's well-drilled defence hard to break down. United's best chance did not arrive until the 25th minute, when a neat one-two between Jason Beckford and Snodgrass saw the United goal machine played in behind the Millwall defence.

Jimmy Abdou scores the equaliser at Elland Road to put Millwall on the road to Wembley after knocking-out Leeds United in the play-off semi-final.

Beckford's low drive was pushed away by Lions 'keeper David Forde, however, who was quick enough to get to his feet and foil Fabian Delph's follow-up. Despite all the applied pressure from Leeds, Forde had had a relatively quiet first period, in which Snodgrass tested the big Irishman twice without too much concern.

If the first half had been relatively tame, it would dramatically change after the interval, when United were awarded a penalty after Andy Frampton tugged at Sam Sodje's shirt in the 48th minute. Once the Millwall protests diminished, Beckford was ready to claim his 35th goal of the season; but to his and the home supporters' horror, his tame effort was easily dealt with by Forde.

This miss added another to the catalogue of spot-kick failures that afflicted United throughout the campaign, but this latest calamity was all but forgotten four minutes later when Leeds brought the tie level. A breathtaking move down the left began with left-back Ben Parker's storming run that took him the length of the pitch, then, after exchanging

Garry Alexander and Paul Robinson savour the moment in front of the Millwall fans after the game at Elland Road.

passes with Andy Robinson, he put in a devastating cross for Luciano Becchio to slide home.

A buoyant Leeds now went in search for the killer goal, pouring forward with one attack after another. Beckford volleyed over when in a great position, then wasted another good chance following a route-one ball. Failure to take any these chances was to condemn Leeds to another season of League One football, for in the 74th minute Millwall equalised to regain the aggregate lead.

The Lions had been frugal to say the least when it came to the offensive part of the game, but this foray into the Leeds half was to prove vital. When Dave Martin finally got some space to exploit by sending over a tantalising cross, to find Lewis Grabban beyond the far post. Instantly the youngster coolly side-footed the ball back into the danger zone for Frenchman Nadjim (Jimmy) Abdou to tap home from close-range.

A blow to Leeds, certainly, and it was definitely not in the script; their assumption, or perhaps arrogance, that the second leg was going to be a

Two shots from the winning dressing room where the Millwall players show their delight following a highly charged 2nd leg game with Leeds United.

mere formality hit them where it really hurt. They rallied briefly, with Bradley Johnson's screamer whistling inches wide of a post, but even in the allotted seven minutes of injury time, Millwall never looked like relinquishing their lead.

A resilient defence led by the outstanding Zak Whitbread, who sustained a serious-looking injury early in the second half, remained unbowed throughout when faced by a free-scoring Leeds team and an intimidating atmosphere. As manager Kenny Jackett said, 'To overcome Leeds, who are a very good team, over two legs is a very good achievement. Their 37,000 fans would be a big crowd in the Championship, let alone League One.' But the only ones cheering at the end were the gallant band of Millwall supporters who dared to venture into the Elland Road cauldron.

Leeds United 1	Millwall 1
Becchio	Abdou

Leeds United: Ankergren, Douglas, Naylor, Sodje, Parker (Johnson), Snodgrass, Kilkenny (Robinson), Howson (Grella), Delph, Becchio, Beckford.

Millwall: Forde, Dunne, Craig, Whitbread, Frampton, Henry (Robinson P.), Bolder, Abdou, Martin, Alexander, Harris (Grabban).

48

MILLWALL V SCUNTHORPE UNITED

24 May 2009   **League One Play-off Final**
Wembley Stadium, London   **Attendance: 59,661**

Given the Lions' record in the play-offs, they did extremely well to reach the Final at the new Wembley Stadium, having overcome Leeds United in two highly charged meetings in the semi-final.

On an overwhelmingly hot afternoon these two teams produced the best game of the three weekend Finals, and a wonder strike from Gary Alexander was probably the finest seen in play-off history. Alas, the game was to end

The Millwall fans making the walk up Wembley Way to the refurbished National Stadium.

A group of Millwall supporters displaying their colours in front of the new Wembley Stadium.

in heartbreaking fashion when Scunthorpe obtained their winner with five minutes to go.

The game began at a blistering pace to match the weather, and saw Scunthorpe take a sixth-minute lead when David Forde could only parry Martyn Woolford's stinging drive for Matt Sparrow to score at the far post. After the early exertions, the game settled down to swing to and fro, with Scunthorpe looking the sharper – a fact confirmed when Gary Hooper smacked a post 10 minutes later.

Millwall hit back strenuously, only to see shots from Adam Bolder and Jimmy Abdou charged down. Millwall were lacking that little bit of quality to counter United's early dominance; however, they should have done better after 30 minutes when Lewis Grabban was found by Neil Harris on the edge of the box. His woeful attempt found its way to a surprised Dave Martin, whose shot beat Joe Murphy but not the covering Dave Mirfin, whose unconvincing clearance clipped a post before going safe. Poor Grabban was having a day to forget, with another miss to add to his catalogue of howlers.

Then a dramatic turnaround occurred in the 10 minutes leading up to half-time. When Scunthorpe took a throw-in deep in their own half, there seemed no apparent danger, even when Gary Alexander won possession some 35 yards near to the left touchline. But following a neat chest control and turn, the big striker unleashed a strike with such venom it is doubtful if any goalkeeper could have kept it out. Murphy's token attempt proved futile as the ball swerved and then dipped under the bar to pummel the back of the net.

Gary Alexander scored Millwall's two goals in their loss against Scunthorpe. These photos illustrate the ecstasy of goalscoring and the utter devastation of defeat.

Two minutes later Millwall were in front. Martin found some room to cross for the leaping Alexander to power his downward header towards the near post. It seemed that Murphy had it covered, but he allowed the ball to trickle over the line.

There was no respite in the second half either, and this is how Finals should be played. If the suffocating heat was taking its toll, it hardly showed, and on the hour the Iron nearly equalised when a corner found substitute Liam Trotter, whose crisp volley was blocked by Forde, before Marc Laird nudged the follow-up to safety.

But 10 minutes later Scunthorpe made it 2–2 when Woolford left Zak Whitbread for dead to find Sparrow, whose feint committed Forde, before lashing the ball into the opposite corner of the net. But the cruellest blow of all came after 75 minutes when Alexander, with the goal at his mercy and the opportunity to score a Wembley hat-trick, contrived to put his close-range header wide, after Chris Hackett had picked him out with a superb cross.

For the 45,000 Millwall fans, the largest club following so far at the new Wembley, the writing was on the wall, and five minutes from time it was duly confirmed. Vying with Alexander for the Man of the Match award, Woolford pounced on a rebound, before sidestepping Alan Dunne to fire under Forde's body. There was still time for Neil Harris to become the hero, but Murphy gained atonement for his earlier blunder by deflecting Millwall's record goalscorer's goal-bound effort wide.

Dreams of Championship football returning to the Den would have to wait a little bit longer.

Millwall 2	Scunthorpe United 3
Alexander (2)	Sparrow (2), Woolford

Millwall: Forde, Dunne, Craig, Whitbread, Frampton (Robinson), Grabban (Hackett), Abdou (Laird), Bolder, Martin, Alexander, Harris.

Scunthorpe United: Murphy, Byrne, Crosby, Mirfin, Morris, Sparrow, Togwell (Trotter), McCann, Woolford, Hooper (Forte), Hayes.

49

CHARLTON ATHLETIC V MILLWALL

19 December 2009
The Valley, London

League One
Attendance: 19,105

This was just the game to get the fans into a festive mood for the run-up to Christmas, and with the generosity of both defences, especially Charlton's, the home supporters could not be blamed if they thought that Christmas had come a week early. The Lions, opposing their near neighbours for the first time in 14 years, came up against an Addicks team on the crest of the wave, with just two defeats out of 22 games played.

Sitting handily in second place, Charlton were looking to make an immediate return to the Championship after suffering relegation earlier in the year. But Millwall were relishing the challenge at the Valley, despite their indifferent away form, in what turned out to be a thrilling rollercoaster encounter.

It was the Lions who drew first blood when Steve Morison, after a slow start to his Millwall career, scored his fifth goal in as many matches in the

Skipper Paul Robinson shows his delight following the eight goal thriller with Charlton Athletic.

12th minute. The quick-thinking Lion nipped between Charlton's daydreaming duo, Scott Wagstaff and Christian Dailly, to tuck his effort under goalkeeper Rob Elliott's dive.

Millwall went two up after 27 minutes when Morison was ideally placed to prod home after Andy Frampton's blistering drive had come back off the goal frame. But Charlton hit back within four minutes when on-loan striker David Moody raced on to Wagstaff's pass, only to be clattered by Frampton's overzealous tackle to concede a penalty-kick. The referee, Mike Jones, immediately pointed to the spot, with Frampton claiming that he touched the ball first, but the official was unmoved. Deon Burton blasted the spot-kick high into the Millwall net.

A further twist occurred in the 38th minute when Charlton were

Danny Schofield wheels away in delight after grabbing Millwall's equaliser at The Valley.

Yorkshireman Danny Schofield's late strike made it 4-4 in a pulsating encounter with neighbours Charlton Athletic

awarded a second penalty. It all stemmed from a mistake from David Forde, the Lions 'keeper, who should have made a better fist of clearing Frampton's back pass; however, the big Irishman lost possession to his fellow Celt, David Mooney, who placed his effort against a post, only for the ball to fall to Lloyd Sam, whose attempt to score was terminated by Jimmy Abdou's check. There was no doubt in Mr Jones's mind, pointing to the spot for a second time. Abdou also reckoned that he got a touch, but to his disbelief found himself unjustly red-carded. Burton's approach to this second slice of seasonal goodwill was to send Forde the wrong way. Millwall reached half-time thankfully still on level, despite some bizarre refereeing decisions.

The second half was barely underway when 10-man Millwall conceded a third, after Sam's cross was headed down by Mooney for Nicky Bailey to despatch a stunning volley into the top corner and put Charlton ahead for the first time in the 46th minute. The hosts nearly increased their lead when

Burton hit a post before Forde grabbed the rebound. Millwall could have waved the game goodbye at this point, but dug in manfully and did not let their heads drop. When Tony Craig replaced Frampton after 70 minutes, the team was rejuvenated.

With nine minutes to go, Millwall's show of character seemed to have salvaged a point when a sudden break by Alan Dunne brought them an equaliser. The defender got to the byline to cut back a superb centre for Dave Martin to lift the ball over Elliott at the second attempt to make it 3–3. But the drama was not over yet; another turn of events saw the hosts get their noses in front again. A corner, taken by Grant Basey, was touched on, only for the ball to glance off Morison's head for a cruel own-goal in the 85th minute.

Despite Morison's unusual hat-trick, Millwall refused to lie down, and Morison quickly made amends as he held off a weak challenge to coolly play in substitute Danny Schofield for a dramatic equaliser. The former Yeovil man waited his moment for Elliott to commit, before skillfully applying the nutmeg for a well-deserved leveller two minutes into time added on. Incredibly, there still enough time for both Schofield and Morison to clinch a most unlikely victory.

Charlton Athletic 4   Millwall 4
Burton (2 pens)   Morison (2), Martin,
Bailey, Morison (og)   Schofield

Charlton Athletic: Elliott, Omozusi, Basey, Sodje S., Dailly, Wagstaff (McKenzie), Semedo, Sam (Spring), Bailey, Mooney (Sodje A.), Burton.
Millwall: Forde, Dunne, Robinson, Frampton (Craig), Smith, Fuseini, Abdou, Laird (Bolder), Martin, Morison, Grabban (Schofield).

50

MILLWALL V

SWINDON TOWN

29 May 2010   **League One Play-off Final**
Wembley Stadium, London   Attendance: 73,108

So Millwall finally buried their Wembley jinx in fine style by lifting the League One Play-off Final trophy – their first victory in a Final at the National Stadium. Having suffered the downside of the occasion against Scunthorpe in the Final 12 months earlier, this time around the Lions were determined not to let that happen for a second time.

This was not just a victory that saw them regain their place in the Championship, it was the culmination of many elements, from the American chairman and saviour of the club, John Berylson, the players and staff, and the fans – not just in financial terms, but also in terms of the vocal support given to the team over the course of the season. The electric atmosphere that the fans created in many games, and especially against Huddersfield in the semi-final success at the Den, would sweep Millwall to Wembley on a euphoric night.

With over 73,000 spectators watching the Final at an unusually wet Wembley, it was a big day for Millwall. The Lions set out their stall very

Millwall skipper Paul Robinson scores the only goal of the game from a Scofield corner.

early on to dominate for the first 45 minutes, and had there been a touch more composure, Millwall could have been far ahead by half time. Much had been made of Swindon's strike pair, Billy Paynter and Charlie Austin, with 49 goals between them, but the duo had been made all but redundant due to Millwall's smothering of the Robins' creativity in midfield.

In contrast, Millwall's threat had been obvious from the start, when Neil Harris tested Swindon 'keeper David Lucas in the seventh minute, and moments later Lucas was alert enough to block Steve Morison's effort after gliding between two Swindon defenders. The probing Danny Schofield put in a subliminal pass for Morison, whose neat chip landed on the roof of the Robins' net. The goal that Millwall so richly deserved nearly arrived in the 29th minute, when Shaun Batt's fine cross on the run was met by the villain of the piece, Kevin Amankwaah, whose header would have ranked as one of the best own-goals scored at Wembley.

Unfortunately for the Millwall hoards, the flag had gone up after Liam Trotter strayed offside in the build-up, but the Lions did not have to wait too long to take the lead – only 10 minutes later, in fact. A Schofield corner skimmed the head of Scott Cuthbert to fall invitingly for skipper Paul Robinson in the goal area. The centre-back had time to cushion the ball on his chest and then nudge it past Lucas with the outside of his right foot.

The Millwall section of Wembley went absolutely mad, cheering, and hugging each other with glee. Negotiating the rest of the half without any concern, the players and manager Kenny Jackett knew that the job was only half done; surely Swindon would offer a bit more in the second half.

As the game opened up, Swindon's first decent chance came from one of their four corners, when Jean-Francois's header was comfortably held by David Forde. But their best opportunity came in the 72nd minute, when Robinson's headed clearance hit Austin, who was instantly left with a clear run towards the Millwall area. Quickly he bore down on Forde's goal; the young Swindon striker had probably decided where to place his shot when

The Wembley hoodoo has been finally laid to rest as Millwall skipper and goalscorer lifts the League One Trophy after defeating Swindon Town 1–0. Also enjoying the moment are Darren Ward, David Forde and Steve Morison.

Goalkeeper David Forde and Neil Harris hold the trophy aloft to share in the celebrations of Millwall's victory.

Man-of-the-Match Scott Barron can not hide his delight at being a Wembley winner.

Its time to milk the celebrations as a triumphant Paul Robinson shares his delight with Steve Morison and Scott Barron. The crutches belong to left-back Tony Craig who was injured just before half-time.

suddenly the ball bobbled on Wembley's notorious surface. Going through with effort, Austin could only hold his head in anguish as the ball went sailing wide of the post.

At the other end, Robinson, trying to atone for his one and only error, beat Lucas to the ball, only to see Cuthbert clear his header off the line. Then Morison could have sealed an emphatic victory in the 83rd minute when he neatly eluded his man on the right, then cut in, only for Lucas to make yet another block. One last thrust from Swindon saw Austin force Forde to concede a corner. The full-time whistle went moments later.

Millwall would now play in the second tier of English football for first time since 2006. It had been a magnificent team effort. Right-back Jack Smith had picked an injury in training, which meant that Scott Barron, primarily a left-footer, was drafted in to an unaccustomed role at right-back, and he certainly deserved his Man of the Match award from one of the local newspapers. Not only was Millwall's pre-match preparation upset by Smith's absence, they also suffered the loss of Tony Craig just before half-time with injury. The Lions were deservedly triumphant, captain Paul Robinson saying, 'The trophy won't leave my side. I've told the wife that she'll have to move over in bed!'

Millwall 1   Swindon Town 0
Robinson

Millwall: Forde, Barron, Robinson, Ward, Craig (Frampton), Batt (Hackett), Abdou, Trotter, Schofield, Morison, Harris.
Swindon Town: Lucas, Amankwaah, Cuthbert, Jean-Francois, Sheehan (Darby), McGovern (O'Brien), Douglas, Ferry, Ward, Austin, Paynter (Pericard).

ND - #0271 - 270225 - C0 - 234/156/15 - PB - 9781780912974 - Matt Lamination